THE
ARROGANT LEADER

Dealing with the Excesses of Power

STEPHEN JENKS, PHD & FRITZ STEELE, PHD

Smith/Kerr Associates
KITTERY, MAINE
WWW.SMITHKERR.COM

Distributed to the trade by National Book Network.

Generous quantity discounts are available from Smith/Kerr Associates LLC 207-703-2314 or www.smithkerr.com

Copyright © 2012 by Stephen Jenks and Fritz Steele

All rights are reserved. No part of this book may be reproduced or transmitted in any form by any means, electronic or mechanical, including photocopying or recording, or by any information storage or retrieval system, except as may be expressly permitted by the 1976 Copyright Act or by the publisher. Request for permission should be directed to Smith/Kerr Associates LLC, 1 Government St #1, Kittery, ME 03904, or www.smithkerr.com

ISBN13: 9780983062240
ISBN 10: 0-9830622-4-2

Text and cover design by Elizabeth DiPalma

Printed in China through Printworks Int. Ltd.

*To our wives, Carolyn and Debbie,
who have always been dedicated to stamping out
any tendencies to puff ourselves up.*

CONTENTS

Preface ix

1. Arrogance in Action 1
2. The Nature of Arrogance 10
3. Causes of Arrogant Behavior 24
4. The Symbols of Arrogance 32
5. The Consequences of Arrogance 48
6. Coping With Arrogance 68
7. Antidotes to Arrogance 84
8. Institutional Arrogance 99
9. Arrogance in Other Places 121
10. Putting It In Perspective 133

Endnotes 146

Index 150

Preface

We have written this book partly because of our recognition that leader arrogance and its dysfunctional effect have been frequently recurring issues throughout our work as consultants to organizations and their leaders for more than forty years. The other impetus for the book was our recognition that the nature of today's rapidly changing world makes leaders' arrogant behavior, behavior that has usually been decried but more or less grudgingly accepted, even more dysfunctional than typically was true in the past.

So why is it so important to examine this topic now? Executive arrogance is a big deal because in the typical hierarchical organization, they hold considerable power over people's careers and livelihood. As such, they get to define "reality" as being what they think or say it is. So if their style is to ignore or reject the views of those around them, they are in danger of making decisions based on a skewed or just plain wrong view of the situation and their system's capabilities. The more they get to define reality, the more important it is that they be open to hearing and really considering a range of information from those around them.

We both are behavioral psychologists who have spent our careers working with individuals and organizations. We are hired to assess situations, facilitate change, solve problems, train, develop and coach individuals and groups to increase their effectiveness. We are brought into organizations as executive advisors and performance coaches. In the course of our work, we have, on too many occasions, been asked to "deal with so-and-so" (insert name of overbearing and self important executive), that is, to provide real feedback and encourage them to look at their behavior objectively in order to understand the impact of things they do and say that alienate, belittle, offend or just bug the people around them. We coach arrogant people; we coach others on finding ways to work with arrogant people. We've worked on larger-scale initiatives where we have run into teams that prove to be ineffective because of their arrogance as a group. The book takes a detailed look at the subject of arrogance to help readers understand it better from a variety of perspectives, and to give some guidance on coping with the arrogant behavior we all encounter.

Leadership roles in many organizations have been populated by people who tend to take an "I've-got-it-and-you-haven't" stance toward those around them. This is due in part to these types of people being attracted to such roles, and in part to the experiences people have when in leadership roles, which creates an inflated view of their abilities. Although understandable, we see this as a very unfortunate pattern in today's complex, interconnected world. Arrogance is a luxury that organizations can no longer afford (if they ever could), either in their leaders or in the destructive, inhibiting climate they set for members, customers and their communities. Arrogant leaders are ill-equipped to handle many of the environmental trends that demand flexibility and adaptability in today's organizations: globalization, re-engineering, organizational transformation, continuous improvement, total quality management, learning organizations, empowerment, self-directed teams, and so on. Arrogant behavior tends to stifle these efforts, since it assumes that "enlightened" stars can single-handedly produce better results than any collaborative or reflective efforts. Arrogance also stifles the development and self-worth of those around the arrogant leader.

It is also obvious that the last ten years or so have seen some very high-profile cases where leadership arrogance has led to some spectacularly negative consequences for both organizations and the wider societal environment in which they operate. We will be using examples from these cases throughout our discussion. These "flameouts" seem to be occurring more frequently, and it is our intention is to help readers recognize and understand arrogance (in themselves and others) and deal with it so that it doesn't sabotage personal competence, relationships, good intentions, or organizational survival.

. This book is written mainly for two types of people: if you are a leader who tends toward arrogant behavior, you may have received feedback that danced around using the word arrogant directly. This feedback can take any of the following forms, and goes something like:

- You need to be a better listener
- You tend to interrupt
- You have "sharp elbows"

- You "should be more inclusive in your leadership style"
- Some people perceive you as intimidating
- You're not a team player.

More likely, you have not received any feedback at all. You may be the leader of your organization and you don't have a "boss" doing your performance appraisal. Your organization may not do them at all. You may not have a confidant or coach to tell you the truth. You may just wonder: "Do people think I'm arrogant? Am I okay with that? Are there things that I should be aware of to improve my effectiveness?" Then again, if you're truly arrogant, you won't care what other people think.

If you're a consistent recipient of arrogant behavior, you've typically struggled with a boss or colleague whom you consider arrogant and you need help in dealing with that person. It may be a matter of how to provide valuable feedback for that person to improve the situation. You may need to learn how to put on the Teflon suit so that their arrogance doesn't stick to you. You might develop ways to work around or through them. It may simply be a matter of getting a toolbox of strategies for keeping yourself grounded, centered and composed when you're with them so as not to incur a career limiting interaction.

The concept of arrogance can apply to individuals, groups, teams, and nations. It's not a subject that is often dealt with directly, and sometimes it's one of those "elephants in the room" that we just want to avoid. We've conducted research on the subject from a historical perspective, through interviews and anecdotes, from a social and behavioral science perspective and through many interviews with those who have had to deal with arrogance, as well as several who personify the concept in their own behavior. Our quotes and anecdotes span many years, because they are meant to illustrate points, not to be an assessment of current events.

We hope this book sheds some light on the subject for you. The crucial aspects of arrogance and its consequences include:

- In the first place, it is necessary to understand your own tendencies toward arrogance and what can be done to manage them.
- Arrogant behavior is a choice and is in part a result of a combination of one's *life situation* and one's *setting* or *social situation*.
- Once in a particular circumstance of reinforcement—such as having an entourage—arrogant behavior can become habitual unless one is aware that he/she is making that *choice*.
- For an individual, a pattern of arrogant behavior isn't a particularly smart choice, since it limits both awareness of reality and one's ability to learn from experience.
- For an organization with leaders who behave arrogantly, the limitations come in difficulty in adapting to changing conditions plus a tendency to lose competent employees who won't put up with that kind of leadership indefinitely.

To briefly sum up, our intention is to expand awareness and understanding of the nature, sources and consequences of arrogant leadership and thereby provide much better options about how to deal with it constructively. We want the book to be instructive, fun to read, and a source of new ideas for coping with arrogant behavior that you may encounter and for recognizing any tendency toward arrogant behavior in yourself. If it achieves those purposes, we will be pleased. In the end, life's too short and today's challenges are too great to have to waste time and energy simply getting past barriers thrown up by overdeveloped egos, be they others' or our own.

THE
ARROGANT LEADER

CHAPTER I

Arrogance in Action

The recent public exposure to arrogance in the corporate world (Enron, Lehman Brothers, AIG, various hedge funds and large banks), in politics (Dick Cheney, Donald Rumsfeld, Paul Wolfowitz, Rod Blagojevich and others across the political spectrum), and even in non-profit organizations (the United Fund scandal as one example) has convinced us that the time is right for a book that explores such behavior, its causes, and its consequences at both the individual and at the institutional level

The increasing complexity and uncertainty of our times may be a force producing enhanced anxiety and a felt need among leaders to demonstrate more certainty than actually exists. This matches with our experiences while consulting to a wide variety of organizations, providing us with many opportunities to see increasing levels of arrogance being exhibited by leaders. We have focused on organizational leaders because their arrogance has such high impact on members and on the organization as a whole: over-reaching; incomplete follow-through; decisions with poor or outdated data; a sense of being divorced from reality;

losing highly competent people who don't want to waste their efforts coping with the arrogant leader; and the organization's inability to adapt quickly to changing conditions.

This limitation in adaptability is particularly problematic today because the world is changing at a rate once predicted by futurists yet not felt by most people until recently. Now it is clear that change is happening faster than ever before. Not only is there rapid change, but the rate of change is accelerating as well. Just about the time we think that we are able to adjust to the pace, there seems to be another wave of disruptive change and we have to recalibrate ourselves once again.

There are many forces that combine to produce the pace of change:

- Rapid population increase throughout the world
- Increasing alterations of the world's ecosystems
- New information technology that makes global connectedness a reality in both economic and political endeavors
- Rapid depletion of the world's natural resources
- Changing expectations on the part of many countries populations (India and China for example)

These all combine to produce the increasingly tenuous "feel" of the times as people and organizations try to get by day-to-day. Arrogance is a luxury that organizations can no longer afford (if they ever could), either in their leaders or in the climate or tone they set for members, customers and their communities. Survival is becoming more difficult in nearly all organizations because, in these times, survival requires better reality-testing, better spotting of new problems, having quicker solutions in response to change, and learning from experience.

The overall feel of these times includes high uncertainty, high stress, threats to survival (both economically and in some cases physically), and challenges to many assumptions. The stakes are high when it comes to responding to what's happening in the world around us, and many organization leaders are feeling the heat of such a high-stakes game. In addition, economic cycles have become shorter, so that a solution that worked in the past or works now is not one that can be assumed to work for the future. It is an open question how long any solution's useful life will be. Unfortunately, a good working assumption is that it will probably be shorter than you think it ought to be.

Consequently, we live in an environment that tends to breed anxiety as a natural reaction to feeling at risk and being uncertain about what to do about it. In many cases, it is all too easy to feel that one's background and experience are not as helpful as they ought to be, when actions that would have been effective turn out to be counterproductive or irrelevant. Because of our need to cope with threats and anxiety about how to manage unpredictable change, someone who expresses self-confidence may be relied upon even when their confidence is misplaced or based on an unwillingness to face just how drastic the situation really is. In a sense, followers reward those leaders who claim to have all the answers and discount the ideas of others. Consider, for example, this description of Enron's Jeff Skilling :

> "He could process information and conceptualize new ideas with blazing speed. He could instantly simplify highly complex issues into a sparkling, compelling image. And he presented his ideas with a certainty that bordered on arrogance and brooked no dissent. He used his brainpower not just to persuade but to intimidate.

> Without question, Skilling's formidable intelligence had a lot to do with turning Enron into a company that was successful—at least for a while. But he also had qualities that were disastrous for someone running a big company. For all his brilliance, Skilling had dangerous blind spots. His management skills were appalling, in large part because he really didn't understand people.... Skilling also had a tendency to oversimplify, and he largely disregarded—indeed, he had an active distaste for—the messy details involved in executing a plan.... He was often too slow—even unwilling—to recognize when the reality didn't match the theory. Over time his arrogance hardened, and he became so sure he was the smartest guy in the room that anyone who disagreed with him was summarily dismissed as just not bright enough to 'get it'."[1]

Arrogant behavior always has been difficult and costly, and has been around throughout the ages. However, there are several aspects of recent times that tend to exacerbate tendencies toward arrogance in certain types of leaders. One is the shift toward more knowledge-based activities as a percentage of the work done in many organizations. Issues and problems have become less clear-cut compared with traditional manufacturing and sales operations, where hands-on experience was likely to be as good a breeder of wisdom as any other source. A lot of today's work is technology-driven, so that leadership now is more likely to be conferred on those who can provide guidance on the complex technical aspects of the endeavor. People who would have been seen as specialist "nerds" at an earlier time are now in positions where they not only solve technical problems or provide leadership, but also control the activities of large numbers of people as well. The explosion of the internet and its flattening effect on the world (see, for example, Thomas Friedman's, *The World Is Flat*[2]) has accelerated globalization and spread influence in all fields more widely than ever before. Arrogant leaders simply cannot afford the consequences of their behavior in terms of its costs—both economically and in terms of global competition.

For some organizational leaders, the news media also play a part in building up their sense of self-importance. Electronic coverage of one's activities tends to provide a kind of "certification" that you are important and inherently interesting to the rest of the populace (who are not generally worthy of such attention). The more that news stories hail your approach and actions as smart, brilliant, the work of genius, etc., the harder it is not to begin to believe that the press releases are describing the "real" you; In the internet age, this tendency is amplified by the speed with which a lot of such feedback occurs—things you did yesterday are visible and public today, and to a much wider audience than was ever possible before. It requires a pretty self-aware person to take such coverage with a grain of salt, understanding that it says more about what people want to hear than it does about the leader's inherent superiority. Microsoft and Bill Gates were seen as unstoppable before the Justice Department and many states' Attorneys General decided to challenge the company's arrogant business practices. Similarly, AOL and its leader, Steve Case, were hailed in the press when they acquired Netscape and then Time Warner. Now, some years later, that strategy appears to have been nothing more than hubris in action.

We have had two clients who were so sure that their technical knowledge would lead them to a superior product offering and cause customers to beat a path to their door, that they completely overlooked massive restructuring in their marketplaces. In one case, the company is one-half the size it was five years ago. In the other case, the company has become a niche player in a rapidly growing market. In both cases, the leader's over-confidence in his own technical vision blinded him from seeing important contrary signals, despite many people's efforts to get him to see what was happening.

People who can provide strong technical leadership often become owners of the last word on everything from staffing to office decoration, whether or not they actually know anything about them. Others' willingness to defer to them on major technical questions gets interpreted as a blanket endorsement of how smart they are about any and all issues. This sort of over confidence is not necessarily a problem in itself, but it usually is accompanied by a corresponding tendency to treat others as if they don't know anything of value. This dismissive behavior is the real problem. As we will discuss throughout the book, the times call for leaders who can understand both the situation *and* their own limitations in dealing with it, so that they can incorporate the strengths and knowledge of others as demands on their organizations change rapidly and unexpectedly.

Malcolm Gladwell described this need well in a recent *New Yorker* piece:

> "Since the beginning of the financial crisis, there have been two principal explanations for why so many banks made such disastrous decisions. The first is structural. Regulators did not regulate. Institutions failed to function as they should. Rules and guidelines were either inadequate or ignored. The second explanation is that Wall Street was incompetent, that the traders and investors didn't know enough, that they made extravagant bets without understanding the consequences. But the first wave of postmortems on the crash suggests a third possibility: that the roots of Wall Street's crisis were not structural or cognitive so much as they were psychological.
>
> Most people are inclined to use moral terms to describe overconfidence—terms like "arrogance" or "hubris". But psychologists tend to regard overconfidence as a state as much as a trait....

> Investment banks are able to borrow billions of dollars and make huge trades because, at the end of the day, their counterparties believe they are capable of making good on their promises. Wall Street is a confidence game, in the strictest sense of that phrase. This is what social scientists mean when they say that human overconfidence can be an adaptive trait. The person who, instead of pretending to be stronger than he is, actually believes himself to be stronger than he is." [3]

We would label this kind of overconfidence as arrogance personified. As the financial crisis of 2008-2009 shows, there were many institutions as well as leaders that showed incredible arrogance. As detailed in the books *The Colossal Failure of Common Sense* by Lawrence McDonald and Patrick Robinson [4] and *House of Cards: A Tale of Hubris and Wretched Excess on Wall Street*, by William D. Cohen[5], a sizeable number of mortgage origination firms, investment banks, hedge funds and insurance companies all became not only greedy but so arrogant as *institutions* that they ignored warning signs that were clearly evident during the prior two years.[6] Therefore, we have included a chapter that explores the phenomenon of institutional arrogance.

As we will discuss in the next chapter, we think it is more helpful to think about arrogance as less a personality trait than a style of behavior that some leaders acquire by virtue of birth, upbringing, or circumstance and that people really do have choice about how they choose to behave despite whatever tendencies they may bring with them to their positions of leadership. This book explores all aspects of arrogance as well as its consequences and some antidotes to such behavior. We also want to be clear that this examination is not meant to be a blanket condemnation of self-confidence or high estimations of one's competence and self-worth. There are certainly many cases where these feelings are justified based on an accurate reflection of both abilities and accomplishments. The trouble starts when such feelings lead to behavior that shuts out or dismisses everyone else's ideas or potential solutions. Put simply, arrogant executive behavior isn't a problem because it's unjustified or immoral, but because it's a dumb way to operate in a complex and changing environment. It reduces the probability of maintaining a healthy organization and achieving good outcomes in difficult situations.

During our research, we went to people who we considered to be arrogant individuals (and others to whom we were referred) and asked them the question "who's the most arrogant person you know?î they thought of someone who, in their mind, was the true example of an arrogant person. We would then ask ìare you arrogant?î Almost to the person, the answer was ìnoî. Truly, arrogance is a relative concept which depends on definitions, perceptions and expectations. We hope that our exploration of arrogant leader behavior and its consequences will add to understanding in all three areas.

As we noted in the Preface, our goals in writing about executive arrogance are (a) to increase understanding of the nature of arrogant leadership behavior, it causes and its consequences; and (b) to provide alternatives for how to influence such behavior both in others and in ourselves. The main topics explored include:

- The nature of arrogant behavior in executives and other leaders;
- Sources and causes of predispositions to behave arrogantly;
- Situational triggers;
- Role definitions and their potential to draw arrogant responses;

- Patterns of institutional arrogance;
- Consequences of arrogance for people and systems;
- Antidotes to making arrogant choices oneself
- Coping with arrogant behavior in others.

We believe that understanding sources and immediate causes of arrogance in ourselves can help us be freer to choose when to play it a little more loosely and be able to hear others' opinions as worth testing, without feeling we have to abandon views that we ultimately still may feel are more pertinent in the moment. Likewise, when a leader is in full imperial mode, it helps to think about likely causes and what response you could give that would unhook him or her from that track. The times, with little margin for error, require some new approaches. We think this is one road to achieving them, and one where you can have some fun at the same time.

CHAPTER 2

The Nature of Arrogance

One dictionary defines arrogance as "a state of overbearing pride or self-importance." Another dictionary defines arrogance as "pride with contempt of others." Flamboyance is not the same as arrogance. Arrogance is self-confidence gone awry. Many books have been written helping people learn to feel good about themselves, to be self-accepting, to be assertive, to stand up for their beliefs. Not much has been written about the other side of the coin—people who need to learn a little humility, to open themselves to the possibility that other mortals may be as good, as worthy, or as smart as they are. The essence of arrogant behavior, then, is a consistently high touting of one's own ideas and abilities and a corresponding rejection or diminishment of others' contributions (almost as if it were a fixed-sum game—if I recognize value in you, I lose some from myself). This stance requires a persistent closed-mindedness that narrows perception to include only that which one already knows. New ideas or competing descriptions of a situation are simply rejected as having no credibility in the face of unquestioning certainty. It is the old saw, "Don't confuse me with facts—my mind's made up" personified.

We want to be clear that arrogant behavior is not simply driven by self-confidence alone—it also includes the consistent devaluation of others' ideas, observations and concerns. A leader who has high sense of confidence in his own abilities without showing arrogant behavior is able to hear, consider and respond to others' ideas without feeling that it reflects badly on them if their point of view isn't always the best or most apt for the situation. They don't expect or need always to be perfect so there's no need to defend themselves from the possibility of such an occurrence.

By contrast, there is the arrogance and bluster that both Gordon Gekko in the *Wall Street* movies and Archie Bunker (in the TV sitcom) portrayed, and there is the more serious kind displayed by people who truly are smarter or more talented than most others, and who thereby become legends in their own minds. Many talented people are not prepared for the fame and attention that is showered upon them and begin to believe in their own press. Sports stars, movie stars, and music stars are often caught in this web as are talented scientists, physicians, executives and politicians. Often, they don't think of themselves as arrogant, but nearly everyone around them is painfully aware of their overwhelming sense of self-importance. Dennis Kozlowski and Mark Swartz (of Tyco fame, or infamy) were described by the New York Assistant District Attorney as having put themselves in the situation because "they believed that they were above the law, because they believed that the rules that applied to other people did not apply to them".[7]

We have an acquaintance whose whole life is built around maintaining his arrogance. He is very bright, and that is part of the problem. His intelligence has helped him come to believe that anything he thinks, feels, or perceives is right and true by definition. He will go to enormous lengths to justify, defend, and explain his superior logic. The fact that he is verbally facile and thinks quickly adds to his power. Interacting with him is an exercise in futility; one ends up accepting his point of view or withdrawing from interacting with him just to end the conversation. Stating one's own opinion and sticking to it in the face of his barrage (when he sees things differently) is not acceptable to him and he will wear you down with his "superior" logic until he proves to you that he is right, or until you give up.

This kind or arrogant behavior is hard to be around. It takes energy from you because you have to decide with every interaction whether or not your own point of view is worth fighting for in an emotionally expensive manner (to say nothing of the time involved). In the years we have known and worked with this acquaintance, we have noticed that many people initially are very much impressed by him. Some of them become his "followers", their admiration growing all the time. They are made comfortable by his absolute certainty about things; he is never in doubt. Others become disenchanted with him and avoid dealing with him whenever possible. He is impossible to work for unless you are one of those who continue to be impressed with his brilliance and superior logic (and perhaps become convinced that you are so inferior by comparison and that it is better to give in to him than to do anything else). Gradually, you lose your sense of yourself and your belief in your own competence because you are constantly giving in to the person or are spending time and energy fighting for your own point of view only to be "proven" wrong in the end.

Ironically, when something goes wrong, this kind of person is likely to challenge you by asking why you didn't see the problem in advance and warn them, or, if you did see it and tried to warn them, why you didn't more vigorously assert your point of view to insure that they heard it. Either way, it is *your* fault that things went wrong! They can be found anywhere. They may be your boss, co-worker, doctor, lawyer, professor or auto mechanic, but the *behavior* is the same. They control you through intimidation and bluster and cause you to lose confidence in yourself. In the early sitcoms, Archie Bunker set the all-time standard for the caricature of this kind of person. He was so outrageous that he often got caught, but he never learned or changed his behavior as a result. The audience sympathized with Edith, Gloria, and Meathead because they could identify with them. We all have Archie Bunkers in our lives, and usually they aren't that funny.

In the extreme, these kinds of interactions lead to the development of cults. The leader gets stronger and stronger in his own and in his followers' eyes, and comes to believe that his thoughts are divinely inspired and therefore not open to any kind of challenge. In fact, a challenge of any kind is put down quickly and harshly. Jim Jones and David Koresh are extreme and very sad examples. Sometimes these people become political leaders or dictators and have the power of government to enforce their views. Adolf Hitler, Idi Amin, Saddam Hussein and Robert Mugabe have provided such examples. When the world sees these people for what they are, these leaders are labeled as crazy, and their followers as weak people who lack the fortitude to believe in or stand up for themselves. In fact, both phenomena are at work. If you are comforted by another person's certainty, it is easy to follow them even when their point of view would otherwise cause you to question them. When they have psychological or military power over you, they can deal very harshly with those who dare to disagree with them.

We want to be very clear that we don't consider arrogance to be synonymous with exuberance, excitement or enthusiasm for an activity or a subject area. For people in top leadership positions, subordinates often defer to such a strong presence by assuming that the leader will always be likely to downgrade or write off anyone who doesn't share their enthusiasm or passion. However, this may or may not be true, depending on both the leader's actual expectations and the situation. As subordinates gain experience with a new leader, for instance, they may see that, despite sounding very sure of his own position, he actually can be influenced during a debate or will come back later with a new point of view from having thought more about the exchange. This helps them differentiate strength of interest or opinion from arrogance for its own sake.

Of course, the opposite lesson is also possible: as subordinates respond to a leader's consistently powerful and unchanging views, they may learn that engaging in an exchange process is futile, even if serious organizational performance issues are at stake. There is no evidence that the leader is ever influenced by others' views, either during the interchange or after reflection. In fact, the pattern seems to be that any reflection that does occur only tends to solidify their view that they are much smarter than those they manage, and to raise questions about the competence (and therefore value to the system) of those subordinates.

There is another particularly striking pattern of behavior that helps us define arrogance in organizational leaders: the constant playing of the "great teacher" role. Whenever there are difficult situations or conflicting choices to be made, the leader defines the process as the teacher/mentor themselves, (of course) guiding the learner/subordinate to a higher level of skill or understanding. It is not that this is not a realistic and useful process—it's essential to development for both individuals and the organization. Arrogance comes into play when the roles are always pre-determined: the leader always requires that they must be the teacher and can never behave as or admit to having been a learner in any situation. We have seen leaders going on about "teachable moments" to subordinates who have been in their jobs for years and who arguably know the local terrain and required actions much better than the leader ever will. (This is in fact a recurring theme on the TV Reality Show "Undercover Boss.") But no matter—for someone disposed toward arrogant behavior, their self-image will not allow them to behave as or acknowledge that they have something to learn from the lesser beings around them.

The original British version of the pseudo-reality TV sitcom "The Office" provided a great example. No matter how far out of his depth in any situation, the boss David Brent (played to perfection by Ricky Gervais) manages to "teach" his minions a valuable lesson and makes it clear that this role must be his and his alone—none others need apply. Some of his patient condescension makes you cringe in its obtuseness, but it's tempered by the fact that we all know actual leaders who are as bad or worse. It's funny because it's true. In the previous chapter, we cited the super-demanding environment in which today's organizational leaders must make decisions and take actions. In a framework that provides a very useful model for understanding such demands, Organizational Psycholgist Edgar Schein has identified four important challenges that the leaders of today's organizations must be able to meet in order to survive and fulfill their missions. They are:

- **The Management of Surprise:** The rate of change in the environment is going up, and predictability of the direction of change is going down.

- **The Management of Interdependence:** Knowledge work is going up as a percentage of the total activity, and the need for coordination of interdependent units is increasing as a result; the parts cannot really operate in separate domains for very long.
- **The Management of Complexity:** Technology is becoming both more complex and more refined, boundaries and roles are becoming more fluid, and the potential for confusion or mismatched expectations is consequently going to rise as well.
- **The Management of Values & Culture:** The rate of change will require readjustments or assessments, diversity will be greater, and people with different world views will need to be able to work together very effectively.

We would also add a fifth challenge to Schein's list:

- **The Management of Competition:** The nature, degree and pace of competition are changing rapidly for most organizations. A competitor's threat to an organization's survival can come from previously unknown quarters, and leaders that gave competition lip service in the past must take it very seriously or their institutions will be unlikely to survive.

These challenges have caused many organizations to reassess their positions in the new global economy, and have led to downsizing, outsourcing, strategic partnering with former competitors, acquisitions, divestitures and other forms of change and reshuffling. More white-collar employees have had to make major changes in their work lives than at any time in the last 50 years. The nature of organizational life today is very different than it was even as little as 20 years ago. Strongly-held assumptions about the nature of work life, such as lifetime job security, linear career progression up the "ladder," and the value of a career strategy based on specialization and being rewarded for it, no longer can be taken for granted. In fact, in many instances those assumptions are being openly challenged and violated. An employee who expects things to remain predictable and amenable to any long-term "game-plan" is likely to become bewildered, frustrated, and more likely, unemployed.

This returns us to where we began. Today's fast-paced, hi-tech environment presents a number of challenges that are qualitatively and quantitatively different from the past. Some people respond to these challenges by telling themselves and anyone else who will listen that there are no problems, only "opportunities" for people as smart and clever as themselves. When you add a strong dose of greed and a thirst for power to the mix, the result unfortunately is often more like the Enron debacle or the banks/mortgage meltdown than a demonstration of superior strategy and problem solving. Today's conditions call for a very different approach: strong commitment combined with great humility and a willingness to be open to new interpretations of problems, assumptions, solutions, and the processes used to reach them.

In the rather harsh spotlight created by the above challenges to organizational survival, a leader's consistently arrogant behavior can be magnified. The increased uncertainty driven by rapid change is often met by an arrogant leader with an ever more tenacious holding on to their preconceived views; and the behavior triggered is a corresponding rejection of employees' attempts to inject more current reality into the assessment of the situation. The increased complexity fueled by rapid technological developments can create a tension where the leader hears and reacts to problems based on their own (inevitably somewhat outdated) level of technical understanding. To do otherwise can feel like ceding the "top dog" position—even though in a complex system, it need not imply any such thing.

Given these increased challenges of rapid change and developing technology, the challenge of greater need for interdependence follows as a way of coping with these challenges. But again, leaders whose world-views center on their own brilliance will tend to treat other potential partners more like servants who exist simply to add extra pairs of hands without messing up the leader's grand plans. The importance of treating values and culture as key components of organizational success poses a similar challenge. The arrogant leader will tend to dismiss those who are truly different as simply untrustworthy or needing correcting, no matter what lip service has been paid to the obligatory politically correct "diversity" program. And finally, the serious changes in the scale and intensity of competition can often trigger the arrogant executive to prove how much smarter they are than those clods who are presuming to challenge the company. But this response tends to focus on the leader and severely limits the extent to which other members' skills and capabilities can be enlisted to compete effectively.

So if these are some of the faces of executive arrogance in action, how do we get out of such cycles—that is, increase the extent to which leaders who are under pressure can remain open to other's ideas and new information without over-inflating and over-valuing their own opinions and abilities? One of our main themes here is that we can't make much progress without reframing the way we think about arrogance in the first place. For the most part, the predominant view of arrogance is that it is a personality trait, ingrained in people almost like a basic instinct. However, we think that this view is much too limiting. It does not describe the full picture, and severely limits the range of options about how to deal with the dysfunctional effects of consistently arrogant leadership.

When someone says to you, "Who's the most arrogant person you know?" a snapshot will appear in your mind's eye. It could be a neighbor, a person where you work, a relative, a parent at your kid's school, a public figure. When asked, people made the following statements describing the arrogant person:

- He's always right
- She doesn't listen
- He always has to have the last word
- The rules don't apply to her
- He's above it all
- We're all just pawns to her
- He thinks he's better than the rest of us

When pushed to describe what they admired about the same person, the following were typically mentioned:

- She's successful
- He gets what he wants
- She seems to be in the right place at the right time
- He's made it financially
- She's really smart

These would typically be looked at as descriptions of personal traits, and the issue would be seen as how to deal with this "difficult" person, given who they are. As we have said, we think that this is neither an accurate nor a helpful way of viewing the problems caused by arrogance. It has an "all or nothing" quality to it—you're either arrogant or you're not, and the question is just how to deal with you.

The alternative is to focus on arrogant *behavior* as the key to understanding the effects and possible alternatives to constricting situations. All of the descriptions above are inferences based on behavior (what people do and say), since we are not yet able to read minds. The key arrogant behaviors that can block problem-solving, learning from experience, and the like include dismissing other people; dismissing others' ideas out of hand; insisting that there is only one capable person (themselves); demanding constant stroking or reinforcement; and demanding and only listening to "good" news that reinforces the view that they're always right.

The key point is that *arrogant behaviors or actions are chosen, not inevitable.* In a given situation, a person chooses a means of acting or responding that is influenced by a number of factors, including the immediate challenge, their role or position (and corresponding expectations about what a person in such a role should do), and their learned expectations and predispositions. Everyone carries within them the capability to respond with either arrogance or openness to the ideas and concerns of others, and each choice has interpersonal and organizational consequences.

We were able to see this choice-making scenario very clearly in a residential training program with which we used to work, the Power & Systems Laboratory, created by Barry and Karen Oshry. Participants lived through several days in a simulated organization/community and then engaged in extensive debriefing to look at the events and behaviors and to learn about leadership, influence and system dynamics. We assigned people to one of three groups: a small group of Elites, who were in charge;

a slightly larger group of Middles, who reported to the Elites; and the bulk of the people who were the Workers, whose lives were controlled by the Elites' policies. Resources are taken from those assigned as Middles and Workers—their keys, their cash, etc. The Elites get to keep their resources. This redistribution instantly gives the Middles and Workers a feeling of being "less than" and sometimes a feeling of helplessness. The Middles are literally caught in the middle between the conflicting expectations of the Elites above and the Workers below. The Elites, in turn, revel in their power and start to behave as though they thoroughly "deserve" to be in that group and the position of power in which they have been assigned. The Workers feel unable to influence the other two groups so they choose to take little or no responsibility for what's happening in the community.

People were asked to fill out a brief background questionnaire when registering for the program. In the debriefing, the participants always marveled at the power of the questionnaire to identify the most arrogant people so they could be assigned to the Elite group; the most wishy-washy people could be put in as Middles; and the irresponsible, less mature people were assigned to be Workers. In truth, the questionnaire had little or nothing to do with these results. People were placed more or less randomly, and it was the situations and the roles people were in that drew from them the behaviors that were then seen as so typical of "those kinds of people."

Of course, people's backgrounds, experiences, and personalities are factors in whether they choose to behave arrogantly in different situations, and some are more prone to do this consistently than others are. But there is a large, under-recognized influence exerted by both role expectations and the immediate demands of the situation, and these also drive behavioral choices. We believe that when we live in times that call for less arrogance and more openness to both new experiences and learning from them, we have a better chance of dealing with arrogance in others and in ourselves if we treat it as a behavioral pattern that can be influenced in multiple ways. Conversely, seeing it simply as a personality trait almost invariably leads into a tug of war rather than an opening-up of options about how to reduce the costs of arrogant behavior.

Unfortunately, sometimes it isn't simply a case of a person choosing to behave in an arrogant manner—it really is a consistent pattern driven by the person's character. David Brooks, the New York *Times* columnist, labeled this character trait as a form of narcissism. "The narcissistic person is marked by a grandiose self-image, a general lack of empathy for others. He is the keeper of a sacred flame, which is the flame he holds to celebrate himself....His self-love is his most precious possession...He is hypersensitive about anybody who might splatter or disregard his greatness. If someone treats him slightingly, he perceives that as a deliberate and heinous attack. If someone threatens his reputation, he regards this as an act of blasphemy. He feels justified in punishing the attacker for this moral outrage".[8] A great deal has been written about narcissism as a character trait and its effects on oneself and others, and it is not our intent to rehash that here. If you would like to look into narcissism a bit more, a few sources are cited in the end notes.[9,10,11,12,13]

Throughout this book, we will explore the sources and consequences of arrogant leader behavior as a means to seeing and understanding patterns that have usually been taken for granted as annoying but inevitable. The purpose of such understanding is to help us frame situations differently and therefore consider more options as we make various choices such as defining roles, reacting to changed conditions, opening up ourselves to new views or interpretations of events, coping with closed-minded stances, and generally taking a learning attitude toward the world rather than one of misplaced certainty that may or may not match reality. It is our belief that no matter how smart you are, in a complicated world, it's pretty dumb to behave as if you are infallible and have nothing to learn from anyone else. There may be lots of forces that push us to behave that way, but the ultimate choices about stance and point of view are still our own to make, and the consequences in today's world can determine personal and organizational survival.

CHAPTER 3

Causes of Arrogant Behavior

Where does arrogant behavior come from? Why are people likely to dismiss others? Some people are oppressively arrogant, others are happily arrogant, and still others don't even seem to realize that they are arrogant in other people's eyes. Sometimes arrogance seems to arise as a kind of occupational training. Many political leaders are arrogant, as are many sports stars, movie stars, Hollywood bigwigs, rock stars, rocket scientists, lawyers, journalists, talk show hosts, opera stars, pilots, and many others. One form of arrogance seems to be based on a sense of entitlement that is related to the person's intellect, position, money, fame, cleverness, or some other factor. Another form of arrogance is trained into the individual by his or her family, school, church, company, or military organization. The line between developing competence and a sense of pride and developing a repetitive pattern of arrogant behavior can be very thin.

In your own circle of acquaintances, there could well be

several insufferably arrogant people. Arrogant people often are disarmingly charming. They often are very bright, which may be one source of their arrogance. It is incredibly hard to be brighter than most people and remain humble, or even to know how to interact respectfully with people whom you consider incapable of keeping up with you.

When trying to understand and cope with arrogant leader behavior, it can be helpful to understand something of its origins. It is often treated as a personal trait like being tall or short, but we look at it as a set of tendencies that are amplified or dampened over time. With this in mind, we have identified some of the primary causes behind people's arrogant behavior. Obviously, there are other causes, but the ones discussed here seem to us to be particularly potent.

It's Taught—You're The Best and the Brightest

Some people have the seeds of arrogance planted from an early age. In our discussions with elementary school teachers, they've reported that some children behave in arrogant ways from the earliest grades. One first grader announced with great pride that he already knew how to read because, "I'm gifted". He really believed he was because he'd been told that so often. Parents, teachers and educational institutions all contribute to helping people believe that they are brighter, more special, or better than other people through the messages they send to children. Folklore has it that one well-known private school tells its incoming freshmen that they are "the leaders of tomorrow; the best and brightest this country has to offer". Many of their students come from highly privileged backgrounds where they have been denied nothing,

26 | THE ARROGANT LEADER

"You are not the center of the universe!"

including admission to this particular school. And the shopkeepers in the town where the school is located tell of incredibly arrogant behavior exhibited toward them by these students. If children are brought up or trained to believe that they are superior to others, they begin to act that way, whether or not it actually is true.

Another example of arrogance that seems to have roots in messages received while growing up is when some teenagers won't take a job because they find most available jobs are ones that don't recognize or take advantage of their superior talents. Other equally-talented teenagers are happy to gain work experience in entry-level jobs flipping burgers, scooping ice cream or waiting tables. We think that the difference between these two ways of viewing the world of work is due in part to an inherent or acquired sense of inflated self worth.[14] Unfortunately, the reverse also seems to be true; some children are told repeatedly that they are stupid, won't amount to anything and don't have talent. Many of those children have as hard a time accepting that they may be as bright and talented as those who are told they are the brightest. Messages that children receive consistently tend to shape how they view themselves in comparison to others. Some of those messages give the child an inflated sense of self-worth while other messages give the child a negative sense of their talent or worth.

It's Inherited

Some families have a legacy of public service, philanthropy, or leadership in business organizations or government. Children in those families often are told that they have an inherited obligation or privilege. Sometimes children of well-known and highly accomplished parents display arrogance that appears to come from a belief that they inherited the right to behave that way. Essentially, it is a sense of entitlement that puts the person above others in their own eyes. Former President George W. Bush's behavior in college, the military reserves and the White House may have been a case in point.

Sometimes, the sense of inherited *entitlement* is an awful burden for the child who goes through life carrying parental expectations that they may or may not be able to meet, to say nothing of living up to their own expectations. We have heard sad stories from people who initially seemed insufferably arrogant, only to discover the pain they are carrying inside is due to the expectations that were placed on them by their family's demands that they should carry on the family legacy.

It's Having the Right Position at the Right Time

In the Kennedy administration, Secretary of Defense Robert McNamara, a former "whiz kid" at Ford Motor Co. before becoming its CEO, recruited a group of bright and talented people to work with him in the Pentagon. (They were repeatedly referred to in media reports at the time as "the Best and Brightest.") While they probably were talented, being constantly reminded of that very characteristic seemed to prevent them from hearing and taking in different points of view or considering different strategies, especially concerning how to deal with the war in Vietnam. They were so sure that they were smarter and knew more than other people that they shut themselves off from information that didn't coincide with their own views. Interestingly, many years later (1995)[15, 16] McNamara published a book that questioned the absolute sense of certainty that he and others exhibited in the '60s.

Ford is not the only corporation that attracts and promotes whiz kids. Examples abound of arrogant people in organizations genuinely believing that they are smarter (or at least more clever) than others and then acting accordingly. The effects of their behavior only become visible when there is a sea-change or meltdown such as the wide-spread financial collapses that occurred in 2008-2009.

The entire sub-prime mortgage fiasco appears to have been led by very smart (and often arrogant) people in hedge funds, major financial institutions and insurance companies who reinforced one another so thoroughly and successfully that even someone as well-respected and powerful as Warren Buffet couldn't bring it to a stop.[17, 18] The investigation by Congressional committees into the behavior of executives from Lehman Brothers (Richard S. Fuld, Jr.), and Goldman Sachs (Lloyd C. Blankfein, Henry Paulson) clearly show that key executives at both firms (not to mention Countrywide, AIG, Bear Stearns and others) engaged in incredibly arrogant ways (such as dismissing out of hand their own analysts' warnings about the excessively risky nature of many of their financial instruments) simply because they could!

It's Circumstantial

A form of circumstantial arrogance can be seen in the behavior of some sports stars, music stars, or movie stars. As they become famous (often deservedly so), they also begin to be treated by others as if they are special (and better) in all aspects of life, not just their area of true expertise. Often their behavior toward others begins to become insufferably arrogant as a result of their privileged circumstances. Newspapers are full of stories of people who have become famous because of their talent engaging in acts like trashing hotel rooms, abusing substances, etc. with the belief that they have the right to do so and therefore can't be held accountable. Recent scandals involving inappropriate sexual behavior (Kobe Bryant, Ben Roethlisberger, Tiger Woods to name only three) seem to happen when those involved believe their privileged situation will protect them. And Charlie Sheen's highly visible break from his TV producers and attempt at a triumphal tour was in a class by itself in the self-regard sweepstakes.

Others in similar circumstances manage to keep a better sense of perspective and humility. Circumstances alone don't cause arrogance, but probably provide fertile ground for it to flourish. Often it is hard to keep a sense of perspective when the

30 | THE ARROGANT LEADER

DILBERT ©2000 Scott Adams. Used by permission of UNIVERSAL UCLICK. All rights reserved.

circumstances of your life keep indicating that you are special and deserve to be treated differently from others.

Circumstances also help determine organizational leaders' tendencies toward arrogance. Executives who are very bright and have high energy levels do not necessarily or automatically become arrogant and closed-off to others' ideas. If such people surround themselves with others who are also strong, then their ideas are tested and challenged, and the role they play tends to be characterized by strong collaborative leadership, not demanding and expecting knee-jerk compliance to the leader. However, strong people around an executive can move on to other situations where they can exercise their own leadership. If they are not replaced with similarly strong people, a downward spiral begins to take place: the executive hears more and more of his own ideas reflected back, and less and less of the challenges needed for a balanced view of things. The leaders then can begin to believe their own press about how indispensable they are, and a sense of infallibility creeps in. The tendency toward this kind of arrogance was there all along. In the early stages, they were held in check by an environment filled with strong people, so that the elements of "genius" could add value and not be overplayed. With changes in the environment, the balance is thrown off and the executive becomes more and more of a force with no counter to his behavior. When subordinates with sufficient strength to counteract the leader are not present, too much power gets vested in the leader and his position; essentially, there are insufficient checks and balances.

We have intentionally kept this discussion of causes fairly brief, since our major focus here is less on history and more on consequences, choices, and how to open up more options for leadership behavior to match today's demanding circumstances. Deep-seated personal predisposition is beyond our scope here, especially since we believe that most executives have the capacity to behave in a variety of ways and therefore have the ability to choose whether to value only their own preconceptions (and in the process dismiss or downgrade others' ideas or contributions), or to at least open themselves up to wider considerations. After a brief look at the use of symbols in expressing or maintaining arrogant behavior, we will shift to consequences and ways of dealing with it in ourselves and in others.

CHAPTER 4

The Symbols of Arrogance

When we try to understand the manifestations and consequences of consistent executive arrogance, one of the most interesting aspects is the use of symbols to create or maintain a dominant position in relation to those around the leaders. If we understand the way these symbols are used, we also have the ability to decipher them and to have more options in how to respond to them.

In the Presence of Greatness

A natural starting point for exploring symbols of arrogance is the ubiquitous status symbol language in workplace layouts. It would be hard to find anyone in today's corporate world who isn't familiar with the trappings that organizational leaders use to send messages about their own importance. These trappings can take as many forms as there are things in the world that can be differentiated: size of personal office, luxuriousness of furnishings, location of one's office, having a closed office versus having an open one, having a window or not, the number of windows, visible personal assistants in the area, and so on.

Of course, status symbols are not used just by arrogant leaders. Most organizations today still use a set of status "standards" as a way of showing where people stand in the corporate hierarchy and to reward people for predictably playing the game as they move up the ladder. In many instances, the person may not even want the particular feature to which they are entitled, but it is assumed that they must have it anyway so that the language will remain consistent and people will be motivated to strive for higher levels on the organizational ladder of success. An example is when a promotion comes with a slightly larger office that includes room for a meeting table in addition to one's desk, independent of whether the occupant wants or needs the table and chairs. Even worse is the case where a promotion requires a move to a more prestigious location when the person knows that it's the wrong location for how they want to perform their job.

These assumptions are beginning to change as leaders seek ways to ensure that their organizations will survive in a world that is much tougher than it used to be. They are recognizing the status symbol process as a "straightjacket" that has applied severe restrictions on the use of scarce space, arrangements of groups, placement of manager's work spaces and the like. For leaders who see flexibility and quick response to changes as the bedrocks of coping with high-change situations, this built-in rigidity begins to look very, very expensive—and in some cases, threatening to the organization's survival. In a number of organizations, this kind of office status language has been declared obsolete, so that facilities are created based on their functionality for getting the task done, not for symbolism and maintaining the hierarchical status quo. In fact, it recently was reported that 40% of IBM's employees work from home or other remote locations.[19] Even though there is some movement toward greater flexibility in workspaces, many organizations still hold firmly to the old assumptions, and executive arrogance is one of the major blocks to questioning them. Even when it can be demonstrated that the status symbol language is holding back performance, the high-arrogance executive will rationalize how important it is to maintain such distinctions, for motivation, morale, external image, or whatever. The common unspoken driver is usually that they personally feel that they must have the trappings of the office in order to maintain a one-up position. Their elaborate workplace visibly communicates how effective and vital they are in the operation, especially with respect to those who don't have such tangible evidence of their indispensability.

We once worked with the executive team of a high-powered financial institution where space was extremely expensive and the layout very status-driven. The CEO had concluded that having a huge personal office (in the 800 square-ft. range) made no practical sense and sent the wrong message to many other valuable contributors who were jammed into spaces too small for their daily activities. He proposed turning his space into a group work area and shifting himself to a standard management office of about 150 square feet.

His second-in-command, the Senior Vice President, immediately went ballistic. He felt this should not be done because it would disrupt the orderly differentiation of senior levels, and would be demoralizing to the whole organization. Some further discussion drew out the fear that if the CEO shifted, the Senior VP would be expected to do likewise, and he felt that he was much too important to operate out of a standard office. He was also convinced that his authority would be challenged more if he did not have the big office and fancy furnishings. This was actually not very likely, since he had made it very clear to all below him that he did not want his ideas challenged in any setting.

The CEO received other, more indirect messages from executives who were uncomfortable with his move. He eventually decided that it wasn't worth the hassle and stayed where he was. He did, however, institute a policy that encouraged people to use his office as a meeting room when he was not in it (which was a good percentage of the time). This has been quite successful because one of the problems of this corporation was that they were very tight for meeting spaces and were trying to work more collaboratively. Unfortunately, the Senior VP's office still sits off-limits to everyone else when he is not in it, serving as a kind of marker of his (self)importance to the organization.

A way to let go...

"A popular current buzzword is "transparency," which usually implies disclosure and honesty, but it also can literally begin with the physical setting and what's in view or hidden. Transparency is affected by the actual structure and materials used in executive work areas, including: opaque walls versus glass, having actual walls (closed offices) or not, offices visible (or not) from circulation paths, common activity areas that are visible from offices, etc. ... For example, a number of years ago Steelcase, the office environments company based in Grand Rapids, Michigan, did away with their isolated (and isolating) executive row of offices and created an alternative "Leadership Community" consisting of all senior executives and their assistants. They all had personal work places that were visible and accessible to one another. They also created a rich mix of meeting rooms, private enclaves and informal areas all scattered around a technology and information-rich space meant to serve as the community center. This had barn-like doors that could be opened for accessibility or closed for privacy. The purpose of this major change was to facilitate much easier contact, information exchange and fluid operation as a team while reducing the need for formal appointments and long informational meetings." [20]

The Seat of Power

A more transitory symbol of self-importance is the location of one's seat in meetings, conferences and the like. Arrogant executives are very sensitive to where they are located, and whether the appropriate message about importance will be sent to others. If there is an obvious "head seat," they have to sit in it. If there is a head table, they have to be sitting at it (and in its head seat, naturally). In contrast, a top executive who wants to get a different feel for a meeting or other event will mix up the pattern occasionally by sitting in a different spot, and listening rather than striving to always control what is happening. The executive who is first and foremost demonstrating his or her own self-importance is not free to do this, no matter how useful it could be to them. They feel that they could lose face (and some sort of points in the competitive game of life) if they did not keep all symbolic messages consistently saying that they are No. 1.

Wheels of Glory

The lore of organizational life contains many other media that can be used to express one's superiority over the general population. A large luxury car certainly can fulfill this function, especially when displayed in a specially designated parking space that is conspicuously close to the entrance so it can be seen by all those who had to take their chances in the general parking lot and trudge to the door. We must admit, however, that we occasionally have also seen the reverse ploy: a very arrogant person driving a beat-up clunker and never missing an opportunity to tell everyone how smart it is to spend as little on transportation as possible and how important it is to be humble like themselves. In New York City, many senior executives are transported to and from work in their own or hired limousines as befitting their status when the actual time to get from home to the office could be much less if they used the subway system like other less important employees. There is no doubt that it's easier to work in a limo than on the C Train, but having a limo and driver constantly available and highly visible also sends a very clear message about a person's importance.

Keeping Up Appearances

It is less clear how homes and other personal spots are used in this way. Certainly, there are executives who use their homes as visible demonstrations of their status and good taste. When making a change of house, they almost always have to move upward, to a bigger house in a better location, with more land (if in the suburbs), etc., even if their family life stage says that with grown children they actually need less space, not more. We would guess that this pressure is greater in smaller communities where people see and visit each other's homes, as compared with organizations based in large cities. In the latter case, people often live in very dispersed locations and scatter in all directions when the workday ends. Even so, the truly arrogant executive probably could not live in a location that was not considered a reflection of his or her status.

Choices about homes and life styles are probably best used as a symbolic indicator of true personal style by those executives who are not particularly arrogant. We know the CEO of a very successful corporation who lives in the same modest house that his family has occupied for more than 50 years. It works well for them so he figures, why change? Similarly, billionaire Warren Buffet's modest house has been his family's home for 55 years. Obviously, neither of these powerful individuals have to impress others with their lavish architecture—they know they have an impact on the world around them Conversely, we have seen executives with elaborate estates from which they got great enjoyment, and that was why they chose them. They didn't care if anyone else knew about or admired their homes or not, which again makes this a non-arrogant stance. *The test is not a modest home versus an elaborate one; it is whether the person feels free to choose the kind of place they really like regardless of the symbolic messages to others.*

The Height of Taste

Office furnishings provide a richer, more direct avenue for expressing one's importance and value to the system (or the world at large). Some high-arrogance executives go in for the traditional battleship desk with enormous surface and little or no flexibility. Wherever you park one of them, they stay put since it takes a crew of six to move them without major injuries. Huge credenzas, massive bookcases, large conference tables inside the office—all of these can be used as expressions of the importance of one's activities. Or they may, in some cases, simply be useful for the work being done. It would be easy to tell the difference, simply by watching how the stuff gets used for a bit, except that the territory would usually be out of bounds to all but invited guests, making it very hard to tell what actually goes on there, anyway.

Where form truly can follow function…

"The offices of SEI Investments in Oaks, Pennsylvania provide one of the most dynamic examples of a new physical and social setting designed to reduce blocks and delays in both communication and adaptive changes in structure or process. The basic layout is relatively open, executive spaces are no different than any others, and most furniture is on wheels so reconfigurations or relocations can occur both easily and cheaply. This set-up also tends to create a shared view that social and physical structures are a result of on-going assessment and re-design, not just periodic major upheavals." [21]

A more savvy new breed of arrogant executive will forgo all the traditional furniture symbols in order to be seen as up to date. Their surroundings usually include modular chrome and glass items, combined with as much sophisticated technology hardware as they can cram into the space. No matter that they usually have not invested the time to learn how to use the equipment effectively…that's for others whose time is less valuable. We had a client who had to have the current generation, fastest personal computer on her desk, so that no one would think that she was not on the cutting edge. The machines were mainly used by her assistants when she was traveling to field locations, so they actually did pretty well on the whole, even though the equipment was not accessible when the executive was in her office.

We have recently seen the emergence of the videoconference center as another technology tool that can be used for important-person play as well as for effective communication. Having videoconference capability can be a wonderful communications tool as well as a time and money saver for organizations with widely spread office or plant locations; and when used properly, travel time and costs tend to be cut significantly. A problem arises, however, when the use of the center becomes tied to one's prestige. The worst case we have seen was the senior executive who treated the Video center as his private toy, to be made available to him anytime he wanted to communicate with other locations. He would pre-empt scheduled product design or engineering conferences in order to have short chats with his peers in the field, no matter how important or trivial the topics. The people who were really depending on the system to shorten development cycle time became so frustrated that they stopped scheduling video sessions and went back to getting on planes and eating up days in travel time. The executive's status symbol was unfortunately also others valuable performance tool that could no longer be relied-upon when deadlines were critical.

The Royal Table and the Royal Loo

The Executive Dining Room is another feature of the traditional corporate world that has served as a symbol of both importance and (unintentionally) arrogance. There are a number of messages to the whole membership implicit in having a separate facility for the upper echelon of management:

- We are too important to eat in the same area with common folk.
- We need to be with "our own kind".
- There is no value in interacting with anyone except people like ourselves during meals; we would never learn anything useful by mixing.

The usual stated function for the executive dining set-up is that it allows the users to use their mealtime to accomplish important connecting conversations with one another. The other messages above tend to be unintended, but are still received no matter the intent. Providing separate dining for executives carries a high fall-out cost along with the actual price tag for running it. The other famous executive perk is the private washroom as a part of one's office suite. We see fewer of these than we used to, but they are still fairly numerous. They, too, send the message that the occupant is too important to have to mix with commoners. The unintended effect is also to reduce the odds that the executive will have any unplanned, casual contacts with anyone during the work day, thereby reducing their likelihood of knowing much about the mood or what's unofficially going on in the organization.

In truth, Executive Dining Rooms, Executive Washrooms, and the like are being questioned more often than not and many leaders are recognizing them as symbols of an obsolete style of organizational leadership that emphasized the gap between the "enlightened" top leadership and the rest of the herd. To the extent that leaders are trying to reduce such a perceived gap and encourage members at all levels to take responsibility for problem-spotting, problem-solving, and exercising appropriate good judgment, these symbols become anchors holding back such a shift in perception and attitude. Even worse, if they are maintained, employees read them as non-verbal messages that the top leaders are not actually willing to "empower" people at all levels, and that all the rhetoric about supporting personal initiative is just that—rhetoric rather than a commitment to be supportive of people actually taking such initiative.

Suckers' Walk

There is a convention in pickup football games called "suckers' walk," which means that after a touchdown is scored, the successful team stays put and the scored-upon team has to trudge to the other end of the field for the next kick-off. There is a similar ploy that is often used by consistently arrogant leaders. They expect (and sometimes demand) that most meetings with subordinates take place in their own office. The message is similar to the football game: the "suckers" who are less important should spend their time traveling so that the leaders don't waste their more-valuable minutes. This serves the purpose of keeping the leader one-up on the others (as does having all interchanges on their home turf), and it is certainly one way to do it. The potential down sides are that it programs a certain kind of deferent and possibly repetitive process into the event, is less likely to allow subordinates to show their strengths, and loses the opportunity for the leader to get out and sense what's going on outside their own well-fortified world. Several of our client companies have had entire floors solely for the offices of the senior executives, and subordinates who were summoned to the heights, when exiting from the elevator, were required to have a secretary buzz them in.

The Royal Procession

Another process-type symbol used by the practiced arrogant executive is particularly interesting...people who surround themselves with a human entourage. People are arranged to accompany the executive to show how important they are and how much deference should be paid to them. The executive primes the pump by moving around the organization with their entourage, made up of people who can be relied upon to provide the correct response to comments, questions, witticisms, and the like. The members of the entourage usually are dependent on the central person in some way, for money, jobs, approval, or reflected status by being associated with the executive. A good example from the old television hospital-based show "St. Elsewhere" was the Grand Rounds tour of the floor conducted by the chief surgeon. Any acolyte who challenged his opinion was instantly put down.

The followers will generally support and applaud whatever the executive does, which can set a good model for others who are touched by the royal procession. This may have its roots in English monarchs' processions with their entourages from country house to country house in past centuries, where the point was to bestow royal favor on lesser mortals by mooching off them. This was supposed to be worth it just for the royal presence itself. But the fundamental symbolic purpose of today's executives is served simply by having the entourage present. Even if its members remain completely silent, it speaks volumes as an example of how visible and important the executive is. This phenomenon also is seen with some music stars, politicians and sports stars—they always have an entourage with them.

We had a CEO client who was so removed from day-to-day work life that whenever he and his entourage were spotted, the word would very quickly travel around the main building that there had been a "Harold sighting." This elusiveness served to reinforce the common belief that Harold was the only person in the organization who had the "big picture" and could therefore keep them on the right track. That view didn't seem to consider how dependent Harold was on what he would hear from his entourage.

Interestingly, the followers often resent the process and will reluctantly go along with the touring only as long as they feel they have something to lose if they opt to bow out. The executive is often blind to this dynamic. Rather than seeing themselves as coercing their troupe into following them around, they believe that people are with them because it is such an exciting, vibrant experience, and is efficient because work assignments can be handed out in real time. They can't conceive of the possibility that some people might have other things to do that are more important (to them) than following a self-important person around. Since one of the basic constructs of the arrogant executive is that it is a privilege for others to have contact with them, allowing that to happen is felt to be a favor being bestowed in spirit of generosity and good will. This is also why the executive is so affronted if someone does say no, or tells them at some point what a drag it is to waste time wandering around—it feels like an extreme lack of gratitude for generous sharing of one's attention and aura.

We recently had a client who attracted an entourage for a different reason; its members were afraid that the executive would (with insufficient information) make changes to all kinds of work in progress, priorities and schedules that they then would have to cope with subsequently. If they were with the executive when he came through their part of the organization, they at least had the chance to curb such changes before much damage was done.

Suitable Costuming

Style of dress is another obvious medium for symbolic identification of self-importance. The typical arrogant executive will tend to feel on display most of the time (since people will naturally be watching) and therefore dress accordingly. Sometimes this means dressing up in terms of formal business attire, and sometimes it means consciously dressing down, with some carefully crafted "informal" look that demonstrates that they are after all, just one of the common people at heart. The prototype outfit for this mode was probably the black turtleneck and jeans worn by Steve Jobs, the leader and dominant presence in Apple. In either case, the same underlying message also is communicated—that this is the "proper" way to dress for our endeavors, and those who are competent would of course emulate it.

For example, we once worked in an organization where most of the higher-level male managers wore bow ties. We finally asked why this pattern existed, and were told that it was simply an effective way to dress for the work they did. When we got to know people better, a manager confided that there might also be another reason. The firm's founder had loved bow ties, and it became an article of faith that those who wore bow ties were more "professional" than those who did not. The founder was long-gone, but the bow ties as symbols of competence remained. As far as we know there has been no research demonstrating the superiority of bow ties in that industry (or any other, for that matter, since executives don't generally run machinery that could snag more traditional ties). The same kind of copycat behavior (among men) often can be observed with regard to face hair; if the boss has a beard, chances are much greater that there will be many more beards among his subordinates that might otherwise be the case.

It's Too Complex for Mere Mortals

In today's high tech organizations such as those that create and sell computer hardware or software, there is a high potential for arrogant behavior tied to technical knowledge. People who have positional power will often dismiss others' dissenting ideas as examples of their lack of technical sophistication. There are, of course, instances when this is accurate, but when an executive is in the arrogant mode, it tends to be a reaction based solely on position and not on the merits of the arguments. One of the symbols of such dismissive arrogance is the innocuous dry-erase marker. We have seen meetings where an arrogant manager would grab the marker out of the hand of whomever was diagramming on a white board, shove the person aside, and proceed to draw their received truth on the board for all to see and marvel at. They would effectively control the meeting as long as they hold the marker, and they would typically only note an idea if it was their own or one with which they agreed.

In these kinds of technical meetings, arrogance can be developed almost as an art form. In addition to the highest-ranking person, other members may take arrogant (i.e., non-discussable) positions about concepts that they feel they know more about than anyone else present. Such meetings seldom result in any new ideas or syntheses emerging, since the main game is simply to claim superior knowledge and then declare as facts whatever points you want to have accepted without alteration.

The high tech example suggests that when it comes to using symbols as expressions of arrogance, one other key point should be made. Every organizational culture develops its own language about status and important person ploys, so that you need to know the language in order to tell what is being expressed. Some of the language is rooted in the nature of the enterprise's business or challenges (hospitals have a different code than lumber yards, for instance), while other components are influenced by the location (e.g., Northeast vs. Midwest) or the size of the system

(Microsoft vs. a software start-up company). You need to have a feel for these factors in order to determine whether someone is using the kinds of symbols we have discussed here to bolster their own sense of importance, to send press releases to others about that importance, or actually to get something done with attention to the culture's symbolic language.

To return to one of our main themes, current demanding times have generally made an arrogance-driven status game too costly and dysfunctional for most organizations. It is too rigid, too set and too inhibiting in terms of quick responses and experimentation. It is almost the prototype cause of non-adaptability in a changing environment. We feel that organizational leaders must be free of their required "look" and scripts in order to learn from experience, to change when it's called for and to stimulate creativity in themselves and others.

CHAPTER 5

The Consequences of Arrogance

At this point, it is time to ask some obvious questions: arrogant executive behavior may be widespread and annoying, but so what? What are the effects or results of a long-term pattern of arrogance? Is this area important enough to warrant time and attention being paid to it? We obviously think that it is, or we would not have gotten so deeply into the subject. To demonstrate why we think it is useful, we will look at three broad areas of impact: on the arrogant leader, on the people around them, and on the organization as a whole.

It's Good to be the King

For an executive with a pattern of arrogant behavior, the consequences of such a personal style are a mixed bag, but there are certainly several positive returns from it, which is what you would expect. If there were not, they would not be likely to develop or maintain such a style into their adult life. Perhaps the central return is the regular reinforcement of one's self-image as the best, brightest, smartest, most sophisticated, or whatever the dimensions may be. Interchanges with other people are geared first and foremost at demonstrating this fact to them (and to oneself), which is why it is hard to give much credit to others' views. To the extent that the person can maintain the arrogant stance and others can't break through it, this self-concept as the best will be confirmed.

Another gain is a feeling of certainty in dealing with the surrounding world. We have suggested that high-arrogance executives may have a lower tolerance of ambiguity than non-arrogant ones, so the occurrence of unpredicted events is not a pleasant experience. One advantage of their sense of certainty, therefore, is that it helps make the world seem manageable and predictable. This, in turn, would tend to reduce anxiety about whether things are predictable enough to be understood and managed. If other people visibly appreciate this sense of certainty, it tends to reinforce the leader's personal feeling that they are the most competent and important person in their world.

The most straightforward reward that an arrogant style brings is that, more times than not, they get what they want in most situations. Sometimes this simply means that they get agreement from others—"ok, you win, we'll look at it your way". Or they are able to influence others and get actual compliance—"ok, you win, we'll do it your way". An extension of this effect is that they can gain control over meetings and other events. They are a force to be reckoned with, and other people must convince them in order for the whole thing to move ahead. We have seen many examples of executives who could literally hold major management sessions captive until the other members would agree that they were absolutely right about whatever issue was at hand. Enron's Andy Fastow provides a good case in point:

> "To the bankers and Wall Streeters he dealt with regularly, Fastow's volatile fist-pounding manner came to exemplify Enron's culture. And over the years, it only got worse. 'As time went on, Andy changed,' says an early senior executive. 'People started to become afraid of him and afraid to speak out. It almost created a fear factor between Andy and people who did not agree with him.' " [22]

Another rewarding aspect of this control may simply be getting attention: "if I am the one who has to be convinced in order to make any progress, it swings the spotlight very directly onto me. My intelligence and credibility have become the real topic, rather than the content that we are supposedly discussing". Not everyone needs or even wants that sort of showcase, of course, especially on a regular basis. But the high-arrogance executive probably needs it fairly regularly as a reconfirmation of their importance to the whole scheme of things in the organization.

The biggest reward for consistent arrogance is often career success itself. If the organization's internal climate includes a pattern of institutional arrogance (which we will discuss in Chapter 8), arrogant executives will tend to be rewarded and move up in the hierarchy at a relatively rapid pace compared with non-arrogant ones whose strengths will be less visible. There will be a cadre of people who are rewarded specifically for their pushiness, thereby sending a message about valued behavior to the rest of the organization. Later, we will discuss whether this is a good thing from the organization's point of view, but it is clearly a positive motivating factor for the individual executive striving to get the top and stay there.

Why Bother—It's Not Worth the Effort

These gains don't come for free, however. We see a number of down sides or costs to a consistently arrogant stance toward one's fellow executives (or anyone else, for that matter). Ironically, one of the largest is that over time, arrogant behavior is a style that tends to reduce one's ability to be truly influential. The more people see you as someone who has to be right about everything, the greater their resistance becomes. They resent the predictable and uncompromising style and are less willing to be influenced even if the idea has considerable merit. It gets reacted to as part of the style rather than part of the issue: "Oh, it's just Phil being Phil..." Or, in a more publicly obvious example, Don being Don: "Shortly before the September 11th attack, word from the Pentagon and Congress was that Cheney's confidant, colleague, and friend Don Rumsfeld was finished at Defense. While most agreed that Rummy had the right program for reform of the military, according to one retired general, Rumsfeld—SecDef for the second time in twenty-six years—was so arrogant and abusive that he alienated everyone he would need to make his reform agenda happen." [23]

This resistance to being influenced will develop relatively quickly if people are not dependent on the executive for jobs or favor. If they are, the effects will still be there, but they will tend to be less obvious. The mounting resentment will result in passive resistance such as omitting to follow-through on agreements or not bothering to tell the arrogant person information that is critical to their understanding of a situation. The covert message seems to be, "if he's so smart, let him figure it out for himself."

In essence, the arrogant style tends to generate a natural distance between the executive and those to whom they relate, even if they have contact on a daily basis. People feel that it takes more energy and trouble to get their points heard than it's worth, and they begin to pull away from contacts with a highly arrogant person. Those who must stay connected because of formal positional demands will do so, but most other people will not. This experience can be somewhat lonely for executives, but they don't usually acknowledge that fact or explore the causes. Instead, they make a badge of honor out of it being "lonely at the top." They use it as confirmation of why they can't rely on most other people, who are not as committed and energetic as they are. What they do not recognize is that the other people may be quite energetic but unwilling to waste their energy in dead-end arguments.

Flying Blind

The cumulative effect of alienating or beating down those around you has a very costly consequence: it becomes harder and harder to get good information for both analysis and decision-making. If you have enough positional power to win arguments by fiat, you will get agreement with your point of view or perception of the world whether right or wrong, and decisions will be made based on skewed analyses or faulty assumptions. The severity of the cost of this pattern depends on the situation. In cases where any action is better than none, there is not much to lose. But when the choices are tricky and the outcomes will be quite different depending on which choice is made, the potential costs are very high. It is also hard for executives to assess the magnitude of this risk, since they tend not to be aware of the fact that people are keeping quiet about their disagreements.

It is basically an invisible process that can only be flushed out by opening up a climate of real dialogue about the interaction processes involved.

For example, Bush Administration Defense Department official Paul Wolfowitz was renowned for his certainty in the face of mixed or unclear data (after an incident of US-caused civilian casualties in Afghanistan):

> "... Maybe, Wolfowitz said, the Taliban had disguised themselves as revelers—that was his hunch about the incident. 'We shouldn't be so passive in apologizing. We should be more confident.' The officials listened in silence, appalled. Later, one of them told me, 'It was almost like he was creating this alternate reality.' With Wolfowitz, self-righteousness had a dangerous habit of overwhelming inconvenient facts. A government official who worked with him on Iraq said, 'Paul Wolfowitz, for all his good qualities, has an unfortunate ability to delude himself because he believes so passionately in things.' " [24]

In other words, the biggest threat to a leader from an overly arrogant style is *the inability to do effective and consistent reality testing.* The histories of over-reaching and collapsing organizations over the last twenty to thirty years almost always have this as a subtext. The leader or leaders did their assessments and made their choices based mainly on echoes of their own beliefs and information, with little chance that disconfirming views could gain any traction.

In a sense, this is the dominant theme for this whole discussion: when you have major responsibilities in a complex and changing environment, you need to create and engage in processes that provide good information and maximize the probability that new trends or changes can be recognized in time to actually deal with them. Behaving in ways that discourage or block others from sharing both data and opinions locks you into a circular process where you mainly get back the same point of view that you already have. This adds nothing to your ability to adapt, and it is frankly not a very smart way to operate. A truly smart person would want to use methods that maximize the probability of having accurate information so that their decisions can be grounded in reality, not fantasy or outdated assumptions.

Suspended Animation

The other major long-term cost of executive arrogance is the tendency of the person to lock-in to success at a particular stage, overplay their own contribution to that success, and freeze the learning from it into "truthsicles" that get dispensed whenever anyone else has doubts about a course of action. This is particularly non-adaptive in a changing environment, since old lessons are not worth much except as nostalgia value. An arrogant stance blocks their personal learning, and to the extent they can control others' worlds, it blocks the development of others in the system as well. And the concept of learning better how to learn doesn't compute with them at all…they assume they are already great at it.

Arrogant executives are therefore unlikely to learn much from their management experiences. They get little direct feedback about the impact of their actions. They can't relate the outcomes of their decisions to specific assumptions and conditions, since much of the data has been hidden from them by others who have given up trying to get their messages across. The result tends to be executive behavior that is somewhat "frozen" in terms of style. There is not much visible pressure to change, and the "this is the way it is" mode tends to be self-confirming unless there is a major crisis and the process can no longer be ignored.

The lack of learning is amplified because an arrogant person's motivation to learn tends to be low. In fact, the basic premise of the arrogant style is "I have nothing to learn from the rest of you, so just be quiet and let's get on with it." Talking about lost learning opportunities to someone who believes in this premise makes little sense, since learning is not the point of the process anyway. As we suggested in Chapter 2, this usually results in the arrogant leader having to always be in the "teacher" role in relation to the "learner" whom they are so graciously helping. We worked with a senior leader who, when faced with a challenge to his point of view, would turn it into a "teachable moment" to explain why he was right and the other person was wrong. As far as we could tell, he was simply incapable of putting himself in the role of learner and had to always be the top dog. Of course, the result was that he very seldom learned anything, not to mention he lost out on many good ideas that didn't happen to be his own.

It Gets Your Attention

We want to briefly consider the impact of arrogant leader behavior on those who regularly work with them. There are a few possible advantages, depending on your position and the situation. The main one probably is that you can rely on the executive to be decisive, thereby reducing feelings of uncertainty and anxiety about what's happening and what to do about it. If you want this kind of certainty, that can be a comforting feeling in the short run, although it remains to be seen how often that certainty is well-matched with the realities of the situation. Decisiveness does have its place, however, and sometimes it is exactly what's needed when time is short and the choices are relatively few.

A second gain is the option to use the arrogant person as a tool in dealing with some difficult third party. We have seen instances where a person was chosen to deal with a difficult negotiating session because of their overbearing style. The goal was to make sure that nothing was given away, which made the arrogant person a reasonable choice. It doesn't tend to work well, however, when the purpose is to negotiate a "win/win" outcome with the other party. This is hard to get to when your representative is so arrogant that the others don't trust their motives and therefore will not work toward common goals or solutions.

A third possible gain is the opportunity to play stimulating games. If you are looking for a good fight or argument for its own sake, an arrogant executive can be a reliable source of such stimulation. One of the ways in which people cope with arrogance is to try to figure out when it can be useful to them, and the predictability of it can be a sort of "design feature." You may not like it, but you can count on it and possibly exploit it to your advantage.

Why Bother—Again

We described earlier the costs to the arrogant leader of wearing out their colleagues and subordinates. The reciprocal effect is also a problem: the impact on those people. The most pervasive result is probably the frustration caused by not being listened to or having to put tremendous energy into simply being heard. It takes a lot of the fun and spontaneity out of day-to-day interactions and makes them seem like chores rather than opportunities. If the pattern of not being listened to is consistent enough, people begin to feel devalued in terms of their ideas, style, ability to think, and the like. If the arrogant executive clearly wields formal power over their job or career situations, they may actually stop thinking for themselves about issues. They basically conclude, "What's the use—let X do it, since in the end we'll have to do it X's way anyway...." Another example from Paul Wolfowitz in the Defense Department: "The cost of dissent was humiliation and professional suicide. An Air Force officer involved in the war planning later said, 'After seeing Wolfowitz chew down a four-star, I don't think anyone was going to raise their head up and make a stink about it.' Less than a month before the start of the war, Wolfowitz had helped to kick the props out from under his own grand project." [25]

If people do not give up thinking for themselves, they have to invest a great deal of energy in dealing with the arrogant executive. Every difference of opinion requires a major effort if any true dialogue is going to occur. Energy also gets eaten up in planning how to bring up or phrase ideas so the arrogant executive will feel that it was really their own idea, and therefore at least give it consideration. Frequent arguments and playing games with phrasing both take away from using one's energy to deal with the actual task at hand. In some cases, this may be inefficient enough to make the difference between effective and poor performance.

Perhaps the most pervasive effect of coping with the arrogant executive is the feeling of resentment about the lack of give and take in the relationship. The process violates what sociologists call "the norm of reciprocity," that is, the unstated agreement that people will be flexible and make compromises in a work relationship as long as they feel that the balance will be roughly even in the long run. I may give up something now, but I expect that you will do likewise over other issues at other times. When the compromising appears to always be done by the same person, the compromiser begins to feel that it is not coming out as a fair exchange, and that the other person has no commitment to making it be fair. That's when, if there is a choice, the person will tend to draw away from contact with the arrogant executive (the "taker"), and only deal with them when it cannot be avoided.

There is also another way in which the imbalance is a problem for those around a highly arrogant leader. The leader's need to have the spotlight always shining on them results in them putting themselves into most key roles or situations. Others have little chance to be seen or tested in terms of their competence and potential. They neither get exposure and build their reputation nor have opportunities to learn from their own choices and the ensuing consequences. This is not a particularly fun way to work, especially if you really care about the content of your job. It is also not a pattern that fosters personal development, and people who recognize this are likely to seek other situations if they have any options at all.

Step Right Up

Finally, we would like to consider a few of the effects that a consistently arrogant leader has on their organization. One of the advantages of having an arrogant executive is that they are almost always willing to exert leadership: they step to the front and provide direction to their own and others' activities. This is not an inconsequential contribution, since there are certainly difficult times when the system needs people who are willing to take the risks involved in stepping to the front. The downside to this willingness is that there may not be a good match between the knowledge or skills required and those actually possessed by an executive who tends to think that they can do anything. We have seen several instances where the wrong person ended up leading the charge on some problem because no one else wanted to take the risk of telling them that for that particular issue they were not the best qualified person to play the leadership role. Enron executive Rebecca Mark was described as such: " 'She came into the office every day,' says a former Azurix executive,' never acting like anything other than the fearless leader who would lead you out of the darkness.' Mark once told this person, 'I will win today.' That quality of unyielding optimism was her greatest strength. And it was also her greatest weakness." [26]

The arrogant style also provides energy (of a sort) to the system. Its practitioners are willing and eager to get themselves involved and express their opinions about almost anything, which provides more stimulus for movement than does a situation where everyone hangs back waiting for someone else to go out on a limb. The person who always jumps in first can pave the way for others' opinions too, if they don't do it in a way that preempts everyone else's rights to be heard as well. We are not saying that those who are willing to take risks or who provide energy by having a bias toward action are arrogant. However, many arrogant people also have these tendencies.

Its Own Reward

If the organization's internal climate overvalues leaders who are certain no matter whether they are proven to be right, arrogant executives will tend to be rewarded and move up in the hierarchy at a relatively more rapid pace as compared with non-arrogant ones whose strengths will be less visible. There is a cadre of people who can be rewarded specifically for their pushiness, thereby sending a message about motivation and values to the rest of the organization. Whether this message is a useful one or not depends on the climate that is desired for the particular organization, and if arrogance is synonymous with strength, then the messages will be consistent. On the other hand, strength does not have to be synonymous with arrogance!

The other consequence of an arrogance-rewarding culture is that it also tends to de-select people who don't fit this model. They may just not like to operate that way, or they may be very concerned about the extra energy that is required to be coping with high-arrogance leaders all the time. The people who have options and the self-confidence to choose to go elsewhere also tend to be stronger performers who will be valued by other systems, so over time, the costs to the organization can be considerable.

Here is a very clear description of that process in action:

> "But to many of those on the inside, the new Enron culture made it, quite simply, an unpleasant place to work. Many who had joined ECT in the early 1990's looked back on those days with great fondness. That Enron had been an exciting, even magical, place to work, where the powerful sense they were changing the world was intoxicating. The Enron of the early 1990's really had felt new and different. But that place was gone. At the Enron Skilling wrought in the late 1990's, money seemed to be the only thing that mattered. Gradually, people who prized teamwork were weeded out by the PRC process, and those who stayed and thrived were the ones who were the most ruthless in cutting deals and looking out for themselves." [27]

Spinning Wheels

This pattern also suggests that another cost is the inefficient use of energy in the system: people regularly having to cope with leader's arrogance rather than with the real problems associated with the task at hand. In this instance, arrogance is a real and costly distraction, draining off the resources of the organization by simply playing games, fighting useless battles, and making end-runs to go around an inflexible person who is blocking action on problems that need all the flexibility that can be mustered. In part, this is because the resentment and lack of give-and-take makes it hard to build a consistent level of trust within the system. Teamwork and inter-group collaboration both suffer as people play their cards close to their chests and make sure they don't give up too much at any one time. This produces a kind of stiffness in internal relations, so that there is little spontaneity in trying new forms of structure or process as the need arises. Rigidity is also maintained by the arrogant executive being unwilling to try new processes that they did not initiate (which could not possibly be as good as their own ideas).

Unplanned Obsolescence

The organization may also tend to be slow in responding to changes in the external environment. If the arrogant executive is in a powerful position, others tend not to be allowed a mandate or the degrees of freedom to scan for changes and report them quickly. Official perceptions of what's happening in markets, the economy, regulatory affairs, etc., all tend to change slowly because the arrogant leader has to be convinced before the information can be "certified" as real and worth being used to guide actions. Arrogant executives already know what they know, and believe that their views are more accurate than the less enlightened people around them. This puts the people around them in a severe bind, as this description of Enron's CEO Jeff Skilling makes painfully clear:

> "In many ways, broadband stands as the logical evolution of the accumulating problems that ultimately brought down Enron. What Enron was trying to do was bold, even inspirational. ... But in the real world, it ran headlong into the reality of a thousand technical, economic, competitive and logistical roadblocks that keep any business plan—especially one so exceedingly ambitious—from unfolding perfectly. ...Skilling seemed oblivious of the practical challenges of turning his latest grand vision into reality and utterly unconcerned with the enormous pressures he'd created.... All this meant that Enron couldn't ever back away from Skilling's profit predictions, at least not without causing the stock to crater. Which left the broadband executives a nightmarish scenario. They would have to somehow manage to build an entirely new industry from scratch in an incredibly short time against astonishing odds. And in the meantime, they would have to resort to creating a portrait of a reality that simply didn't exist." [28]

Along with slowed responses to specific changes, general learning about the world and what works is also hampered. If reality-testing takes a lot of energy (convincing the boss to consider a different view), energy has to go into building each case rather than into trying to understand what the data means and what can be learned from experience. Arrogance tends to skew the timing of both action and learning, mostly due to the built-in delay of getting past the arrogant executive's threshold of resistance. This timing may be unimportant in some cases, but in others it could make the difference between taking timely action and arriving after the parade has passed by.

Shaping One's Life Journey

Ultimately, a consistent pattern of arrogant behavior also tends to shape the choices and resulting path that we follow as we go through our careers. This is illustrated well by the pattern of one of our clients whom we will call Michael. Michael is very bright. He excelled in school and completed both an M.D. and a Ph.D. in biochemistry before he was 30 years old. He also could be charming. He impressed his advisors, and arranged a post-doctoral association with a world famous researcher who later sang his praises. The recommendations were strong enough that Michael was offered a senior scientific position in a major pharmaceutical firm, essentially leapfrogging others his age.

After three years of very visible contributions, he was approached by a search firm to join a young biotech firm as Vice President of Research. In this capacity, he was able to recruit and hire a number of very talented scientists whose collective abilities enabled the biotech firm to achieve substantial success with their first product. When Michael's views were not instantly adopted by those he had essentially hired, he became frustrated, and after three years, he left the biotech firm to join a major pharmaceutical firm to help establish a new biotechnology division.

In his new position, Michael was given all the resources he needed, and the freedom to pursue promising lines of science with the full support of senior management. In fact, Michael and his team were able to help the firm win FDA approval of a new biotech drug therapy in record time. During this time, Michael learned a lot about the business side of the pharmaceutical industry through his involvement in drug development, clinical testing, the approval process, manufacturing and marketing of the product, etc.

When he wasn't made a corporate Vice President according to his internal timetable, Michael decided to leave the major pharmaceutical firm to become President of a biotech start-up firm. At the time Michael joined, the firm numbered 19 people. Over the following seven years, the firm grew to nearly 200 people before falling back to less than 100. The failure of the firm to reach its potential is in no small part due to Michael's increasing arrogance.

The string of stellar successes in Michael's life (school, graduate and post graduate education, the first three jobs) each added to an increasing sense of his own genius. By the time Michael became President of the biotech start-up, he was convinced that he knew enough about all aspects of biotechnology that he could create a real winner in record time. The actuality was that the product area the start-up was pursuing was new territory that required cooperative input from several disciplines including biology, chemistry, engineering, and surgery. The product was not only a new drug, but one that would be delivered in an entirely new fashion to the patient. There was no way that any one person or discipline could have enough relevant knowledge and skill to make all the decisions. A correct decision in one area often was incorrect when coupled with the requirements of another area. The only way the product could be developed successfully was through intense cross-disciplinary teamwork.

The company was divided into two scientific groups, those that were biologically based in one group and all others in another group. Success depended on the collaboration between the two groups. Michael began his term as president by leading the scientific work personally. His knowledge and charisma helped to pull people together. Over time, as it became apparent that even Michael did not know enough personally to make all the decisions, people began to lobby him with their point of view. Michael began to favor one side over the other, not because of the logic of their position, but because that side was better at "playing" Michael than the other side was. The company developed various cliques that each had a champion…there was no consistent focus. The necessary teamwork never happened, and the company experienced one scientific failure after another. In effect, there was no genuine leadership. Michael blamed everyone but himself for the failures.

What went wrong? In the first place, on his arrival, Michael stated what he wanted to create in terms of a team environment and a focus on cross-disciplinary collaboration. He then acted as the sole decision-maker on the belief that he knew better than anyone else what the right course of action was. He ridiculed those who disagreed with him, and favored those who agreed with him. As time went by, people began to believe that it was futile to try to change Michael's mind and so they focused on their own narrow scientific areas with little regard for how their work fit with others' endeavors. Crucial information was not shared in cross-departmental meetings. Communication with Michael became largely a hub-and-spoke arrangement where Michael was the hub, and each of the spokes lobbied him for their own advantage. Michael never realized that he could not reach the right decisions in such a manner, so decisions were made that ultimately were proved to be wrong. This scenario could have been avoided had Michael believed that he didn't know everything, had he led a process of mutual cross-disciplinary teamwork and the discovery of solutions that built on that teamwork.

In the end, Michael declared that his talents could be deployed better elsewhere, and he left the company. The environment he created (functional silos with little collaboration and the expectation that the genius at the center of things will make all the decisions) has left the company alive but permanently damaged. Once a culture is in place, it is very difficult to change it. His impact on the culture of each of his stops was similar, and consistent with the impact on his own career path: he was never really free to try alternative leadership styles that might have allowed him to learn and grow within a system, so he always needed to move on.

Big Effects

In summation, arrogant executives' styles produce a mixed bag of effects for them, the people around them, and the organization as a whole. There is some energy and excitement produced by their drive, tempered by a tendency for others to give up after a while and actually put less energy into trying to figure out what needs doing. There is some decisiveness and certainty provided by their sureness that they know what's right, tempered by difficulties that can occur when they happen to be both certain and wrong.

However, three key processes tend to suffer under a pattern of high executive arrogance:

1. *Reality Testing* suffers because it is hard for the arrogant executive to get a true picture of what's happening inside and outside the organization. Their need to know everything coupled with discouraging others' ideas of information tends to create a stable but inaccurate picture of the current situation. This is not a good design feature in a changing environment.
2. *Creative Problem Solving* is the second casualty of prolonged leader arrogance. Even if the need for change is recognized, the leader's certainty will tend to steer analyses and potential solutions toward what they already know and believe to be the best approach. Other approaches are

often put down as the product of inferior experience or reasoning powers.

3. *Learning from Experience* suffers because of both of the above effects. Arrogant leaders assume they have little to learn but much to teach others. It is therefore very hard to have the free examination of events and their causes which can lead to relevant learning that can be applied quickly in a process of continuing adaptation. It is also hard to create and learn from experiments when the most powerful people feel there is no point because there's nothing to learn.

If you believe, as we do, that the world has become more complex, uncertain and interdependent, being hampered in these processes is no small thing. The chances of surviving, much less prospering, are significantly reduced if an organization isn't good at them. There may be some "up" periods, but they will tend to occur in spite of the arrogant climate, not because of it.

CHAPTER 6

Coping With Arrogance

What, if anything, is needed in the way of a response to the kinds of concepts and processes we have been describing? There are really two different parts to this question. One is coping with arrogant executive behavior in an effective and non-destructive manner. The other is coping with tendencies toward arrogance within your own self. This chapter will discuss dealing with arrogance in others, and Chapter 7 will look at ways of handling one's own potentially arrogant behavior toward other people.

We should start by noting that there is really no "magic bullet" for coping with a leader whose behavior tends to be arrogant, bullying or both. It is harder to provide remedies for dealing with an arrogant boss than it is to suggest ways of toning down your own tendencies toward arrogant behavior. This is a fairly obvious point, since you control your own fate but not the responses of others. You can choose to try new approaches, such as listening to others' opinions before telling them why they're wrong or even test out the possibility of changing your opinion if the evidence is strong enough. As we'll discuss in the next chapter, you can opt for these as ways to do better reality testing, obtaining more cooperation from others, and making better decisions based on a more clear view of the context. But it is definitely harder to get someone else to try these experiments if they don't see any need to do better.

So, with these caveats, how do you deal with a high-powered leader whose approach to any problem or issue is typically centered on their view of themselves? Is it really possible to collaborate in a satisfying way with an executive who seems to need to see themselves as the fount of all wisdom, relegating everyone around them to bit-player status? We think so, but it requires some very specific and conscious choices in order to have an effective strategy and not get caught in repetitive cycles of demeaning encounters, resentment and frustration.

At a very fundamental level, the first suggestion is to not take an arrogant boss's put-downs personally. This may sound a little strange and hard to do when being ignored or repeatedly criticized, but the point to remember is that this behavior is driven by the needs of the boss, not by your actual ability or level of competence. That's not to say that you're always right yourself, only that it's a rigged game with the boss always claiming the right to judge themselves to be right and see others' views as sub-standard. If you let these interchanges define your own self-worth, you have little chance of doing good work or growing in the process. Beyond this basic point, we see three key factors that should influence the options you consider: your goals in responding, your position or role in relation to the arrogant executive, and the immediate situation or task with which you are trying to deal.

Picking Your Battles

The first factor to focus on is one's immediate goal. By this, we simply mean that it is very important when feeling frustrated with an executive's arrogant behavior that you ask yourself what you really want to accomplish through your actions and reactions. It may be tempting just to let fly and express your frustration, or clam up and do nothing, but neither extreme is necessarily going to get you what you want. That's why it helps to think clearly about what you would like as an outcome, and then to do those things that are most likely to achieve that result. It is pretty simple stuff, we admit, but not so easy to do when you're feeling consistently put down and itching for revenge. The typical tendency for most of us is to get caught up in knee-jerk reactions and useless diversionary games that eat up time and energy while perpetuating the problem. Whether that will achieve what needs to be accomplished is the question, and remembering to ask that question when the irritation is rising may help you to be aware that you have choices about how to respond.

One-Shot Wonder

Of course, taking your best shot does represent one possible goal: simply feeling better. You can dig in your heels, toss back some sarcastic remark, or just refuse to go any further in the discussion. To some degree, you are getting revenge by giving back exactly what you feel you're getting from the other person. Unfortunately, this strategy is often a dead-end move, making it unlikely that there can be a continuing effective working relationship (or, in extreme cases, a continuing job for yourself).

When things get to this point, the tendency is for each person to spend as little time as possible with the other. Not much can be done in a collaborative fashion, since the purpose served by contact seems mainly to provide dueling opportunities to demonstrate superiority. As the job comment hints, this also is not a strategy that can easily be pursued if the arrogant executive has career power over you and you are required by your role to work with them somehow.

Mounting a Change Project

A second possible goal to pursue is to establish a better balance in the processes that go on between the two of you, so that the relationship feels like there is a more fair give-and-take exchange. You may want to try to change the arrogant executive's behavior pattern, especially in situations where you are involved. Your sense is that the costs of dealing with such arrogance are consistently and predictably too high and getting in the way of almost anything you are trying to accomplish. If so, it is worth attempting to influence the other person's style, so you don't start over again with every encounter. This is a very different outcome from simply demonstrating that you can be as arrogant as the executive. You are attempting to achieve balance by lowering the amount of arrogance in the whole process rather than increasing your own component to match the other person's.

A first step involves some sort of *unfreezing* phase, where you try to send a clear message to the arrogant executive about the pattern of behavior and your perception of its consequences on you, other people, and the work process. You need to be explicit about what you see, your standards for evaluating it, and your hopes in terms of the kind of balanced process that we discussed earlier. It helps if you can articulate a desired process that involves both of you meeting the standards, not just the other person. If you don't do this, your approach can be rejected as self-serving and having no value for the executive. You also need to be willing to be honest and confronting without being combative. Your goal is not an exciting fight, but a shared recognition that there may be value in changing behavior.

One model for the unfreezing step comes from the human resource management field: the 360° feedback exercise, where an executive receives descriptive feedback from peers, subordinates, and superiors (if there are any in the system). This can be an eye-opening experience, especially if very different observers provide similar themes about the subject's overbearing behavior and its consequences for the organization and the people around him. Of course, this process requires that the executive be willing to engage in it in the first place, which is not always the case. This is more likely to happen if there have been some unsatisfactory and disconfirming outcomes from the executive's unilateral decisions or by their turning a deaf ear to others' views.

In the *changing* phase, the executive may or may not ask for explicit suggestions about things to try. If they do, it is an opening to suggest concrete experiments that can be tried and evaluated for impact. In our experience, this has a much higher chance of leading to real change than does simply telling someone to be different. You need to be clear that there are specific actions with specific consequences that are critical. Treating the changes as exploratory allows you to play a role in giving feedback about whether the behavior was actually different and what difference it made to the work process. (We could also suggest that you give them a copy of this book's Chapter 7 to use for ideas about things to try. For that matter, giving them the whole book might be helpful toward some unfreezing and an interest in the topic and the impact of their own behavior. However, even we would have to admit that this is only a good idea if the relationship is pretty strong ...You could always leave it on the desk anonymously!)

An example of this trial process is the "active listening" approach, which has been around for many decades. At its base is a commitment on the part of the executive to suspend responding to someone's ideas (and "setting them straight") until they have been able to restate the idea to the other person's satisfaction. This requires that the other person really be listened to, and often that is the first step to actual consideration (versus knee-jerk dismissal) of the idea itself.

For *refreezing*, try to provide positive reinforcement when the leader's non-arrogant actions allow a freer examination of alternatives or a better definition of the problem. Let them know that you appreciate those actions, thereby providing incentives for greater tolerance (rather than the dreaded feeling of not looking smart if they don't automatically have the answers). The best situation would probably be to highlight an instance when the executive set a tone of more open-mindedness that led to real success on a task or project.

One way to do this is simply to be firm about your own opinions. You don't get yourself into a fighting mode, but you don't let yourself be cowed or shouted down, either. What you're trying to do is establish some new norms about how the relationship should work. Rather than being more arrogant yourself, you want to listen and pay attention to the other person's ideas, but you are also explicit about expecting that the other person pay attention to your ideas as well. You are, in effect, modeling behavior that you expect from both of you.

Since what's being considered here is basically the transactional process occurring between you and the executive, a good guide for thinking about it is Eric Berne's classic analysis, *Games People Play*.[29] In his terms, you are trying to restructure your interchanges from a Parent-to-Child mode (guess who's which) to an Adult-to-Adult mode. Keeping this in mind helps you keep focused on choices rather than simply acting out your feelings of irritation.

This approach is not likely to have instant impact. It won't work magic right away, but it is worth staying with for the longer-term. Arrogant executives often end up with greater respect for people who don't cave in to them, even though they may not like it the first few times a confrontation occurs. They grow to see the other person as a force to be reckoned with, as well as a source of ideas (if they can grudgingly admit that other ideas could occasionally be useful). Your strategic intent is to demonstrate competence by confidence, actions and outcomes, not by reactive claims about who's smarter than whom. Over time, this process is more likely to take root if you are in a position or role where the arrogant executive is required to deal with you in order to fulfill their own roles. If this is not the case, it is hard to get them to pay attention or stay in contact once you have stopped playing the subservient role, so there may not be enough time for the balanced relationship to develop.

Having suggested particular change goals and moves, we are still well aware that there are organizations and leaders where such challenges are tantamount to "insubordination," even when the system badly needs such behavior. The term that we often hear in such conditions is avoiding the career limiting move, or CLM. We certainly are in no position to suggest that everybody should ignore basic survival concerns and leap into the fray to straighten-out some higher-up. No good probably ever came from that, and it reminds us of the old story about Hollywood movie mogul Darryl F. Zanuck. He would pitch a new movie idea of his own to his underlings in a staff meeting, saying encouragingly "I want to hear what you really think of this idea, even if it means losing your jobs." Actually, using humor such as that story can be a way of getting the message across when the boss is becoming particularly overbearing. If there is some shared story such as that (or, even better, from the lore of your own system), you can use it to signal when the interaction is tipping over into a caricature of such arrogance.

Helping Others

If your goal is not your own balanced relationship with the arrogant executive but rather someone else's, you have to think in terms of being in a mediator role. Slowing down the interaction process may give the one-down person a chance to get their ideas in before the executive takes agreement for granted and things move on. If the person works for the executive and is therefore dependent on their goodwill, they usually feel that they have a lot to lose by rocking the boat. It may take a third party to be able to suggest a more considered approach that allows more points of view to be considered.

It may also help to talk to the subordinate person one-on-one, away from the relationship with the arrogant executive. You can help them see that they are not alone, and that others also have some frustrations with getting through the stone wall of certainty. This can't become too much a part of the process, though, or you end up creating a closed system of commiseration that doesn't lead to anything but letting off steam. The commiserating should be accompanied by discussing concrete next steps: what options are available and what does the person plan to do?

Just Do It

A third practical goal is simply to focus on the task or problem at hand and try to get the best possible outcome from how it is handled. The key approach here is to be as data-centered as possible. Focus on data, not pronouncements. Be clear about what information is not known, and what is needed in order to make a good decision or do the job at hand. Don't let the arrogant executive skip over this part because they think they already know everything that's worth knowing. Be clear that you are treating their pronouncements as important opinions but not as facts or received wisdom. An important aspect of this approach is to do your homework consistently, spending time on background information and mining whatever sources could provide clues as to the best approach to a problem. It can take more work, but the payoff can be large. Again, the point is to frame the issue around what data will help you make a good decision, not on who's smarter or more clever.

In this mode, it also helps to assess the importance of a finely-tuned decision—are the outcomes likely to be quite different depending on which course of action is chosen? If there is not likely to be much variation, it's probably not worth it to fight the arrogance battle here, especially if you work for the arrogant executive in question. Going along can save energy and "points" for those situations where the outcome really is crucial and dependent on an open-minded analysis. In this latter situation, it's important to stick with the process, since the actions can misfire and be quite costly. You may also get blamed if this happens, since arrogant people are not noted for taking the blame for mistakes. The more likely refrain is "My concept was perfect but you people didn't carry it out right."

The basic approach, then, is to try to base conclusions on what's observable, not on just opinions. This is sometimes hard to do, especially when someone in authority is saying that there's no need to gather information at all. As we suggested, in most instances you may have to think ahead and do some "bootleg" data collecting ahead of the confrontation. Timing makes all the difference here, because if you don't have it then, it will be too late.

Staying focused on the straight task goal above all else calls for managing your irritation and frustration with the executive's arrogant behavior. It may be momentarily (and greatly) satisfying to lash out, but it is also likely to block achieving the short-term goal. Grappling over the other person's inflated self-image just eats up time and energy while reducing the likelihood that they will cooperate in areas where they need to follow-through themselves.

What's My Line?

There is a second key factor to keep in mind when assessing the options we've been considering: what's the role you play in relation to the arrogant executive? If there is a competitive or mistrusting relationship, there may not be many degrees of freedom to try these options. In a similar vein, the more dependent you are on the executive for structure, permission, and career choices, the tougher it may be to have any meaningful influence on the arrogant style. One of the typical characteristics of an arrogant approach is that people are dealt with according to categories—e.g., as worth listening to and not worth listening to. Subordinates can all too easily be written-off as "unenlightened" and treated only as objects to be influenced. You can usually tell this is happening when code words are used to describe why you are not worthy of being listened to: immature, junior, unsophisticated, unseasoned, naive, etc. These all serve to keep you one-down and keep the executive in the role of being the sole judge of competence and appropriate behavior.

If you are in this type of role relationship, your best strategy may be to try to develop credibility with others in the organization through effective partnering or support, and then use this credibility to get the executive in question to reconsider their assumptions or judgments about you. An external source can influence them in instances where you cannot because you aren't listened to in the first place. If you are in a more balanced power situation, you obviously have more options about how to articulate what you see happening and communicate how you would like the process to be different. This is an easier situation in terms of getting the person's attention, but there are still some tricky aspects to it. For instance, the arrogant person's self-image will be threatened by having their behavior challenged, and this may make them close up and not listen to the content of what's being said. They will respond mainly to the feeling of being under attack, which can make them even less likely to be open-minded while doing the task at hand. Therefore your result may be the opposite of what you intended.

A good basic rule of thumb to follow in this situation would be: *try not to be arrogant in the way you confront another person's arrogance.* In other words, give them credit for their own ideas, making it clear that there are things you value about their approach or intentions. Let them know that you place real value on working with them, and that this is why you are bothering to try to work on the relationship.

If the supportive approach just isn't able to connect, you may have to play a tougher game. This would be to make clear to the arrogant person exactly what you are prepared to do if they are not willing to treat the process between you as more give-and-take. Your main option is to withhold your own participation, which is only credible if you have the freedom to make that choice without serious damage to your own career. You are essentially declaring a limit or boundary on what you are willing to cope with in order to remain involved in the system., just as you would for other factors (impact on health or family, ethical challenges, etc.).

Even with these efforts, trying to counter regular dysfunctional arrogant behavior as an individual is usually a low-power, high-risk game. A more systemic approach may be needed, especially if there is a pattern of high-level arrogance in the organization. In a very thoughtful *NY Times* Op-Ed piece, an oncology nurse named Theresa Brown suggested what's needed to cope with a pattern of condescension and bullying by doctors:

> "What can be done to counter hospital bullying? For one thing, hospitals should adopt standards of behavior and apply them uniformly, from the housekeepers to the nurses to the president of the hospital. And nurses and other employees need to know they can report incidents confidentially. ... But to be truly effective, such change can't be simply imposed bureaucratically. It has to start at the top. Because hospitals tend to be extremely hierarchical, even well-meaning doctors respond much better to suggestions and criticisms from people they consider their equals or superior. I've noticed that doctors otherwise prone to bullying will become models of civility when other doctors are around. In other words, alongside uniform, well-enforced rules, doctors themselves need to set a new tone in the hospital corridors, policing their colleagues and letting new doctors know what kind of behavior is expected of them." [30]

The point she is making is related to one of the most important recommendations we can make: it's much more likely to effect real change if arrogance and condescension in high-status people are treated as problems in systemic patterns, not just as the need fix X or Y who's having a toxic effect on those around them. Their behavior has a potentially highly negative impact on the fortunes of the enterprise and is not just an irritant to a series of individuals trying to work with them. The fact that a person who is extremely arrogant was placed in such a high position is also a reflection on the operational criteria that are being used—criteria that bear examination in themselves. The idea is to get you out of focusing on one aberrant person (which inherently creates defensiveness and possibly counter-attack) and into treating civil behavior as what it is: a necessary condition for a work culture where trust and teamwork are essential for dealing with complex and demanding situations. There needs to be some agreement in the organization (and at the top, even if it doesn't include the problem boss) that survival and organizational health call for a climate that expects mutual respect, inquiry and free interchanges at all levels. The problems with any particular boss should be raised in this context rather than a series of one-on-ones where each subordinate can be seen as just whining because they're not getting their way, and are easily dismissed. And the values need to be clear that people should be heard and considered as members of the community, rather than having executives that must always get their way.

Context and Getting On with It

The third major factor in deciding how to respond to executive arrogance is the immediate situation itself. There are times when the immediate task or problem requires immediate action—any action—or the opportunity to make a difference will be lost. In this case, it probably makes most sense simply to get on with it and not use any energy or attention on behavioral issues, no matter how irritating they might be. We don't recommend this as a long-term strategy, but it does have its uses. If you feel that short-term survival is the main issue, then do what it takes in the moment. However, you need to be restrained in how frequently you make that assessment, since it can be tempting to avoid tough choices by declaring every challenge to be an unusual emergency situation.

A similar pressure may be felt when an open confrontation of personal behavior would be so different from the norms you have established between you that it would require a major change effort just to make it discussible. This is not an easy problem to get at, and if you think this is the case, you need to be considering working first on changing the norms about what it is all right to discuss with one another. Involving other people in this process is more likely to be effective (and be listened to) than simply doing it one-on-one. In a sense, you want to change it from being just your personal concern to a shared issue about group process that affects everyone.

The best situation from the standpoint of coping with an executive's arrogance is when the behavior is fresh, the stakes are not too high, and there is not an audience that the executive wants to impress or in front of whom they want to avoid being embarrassed. Then there is no excess weight attached to the executive accepting and responding to your concerns. On the other hand, a situation with other people present can actually help if they are trusted by the executive, they share your views about the impact of the arrogant behavior, AND they are willing to stand up and be heard on the issue. This helps you to broaden the discussion beyond your own personal preferences or competence, which both reduces the risks and makes it more likely that you will be heard.

Ultimately, there will still be instances where the options for how to cope with an arrogant executive are very few and relatively poor. Your role is too dependent, you have too little power, there is too little support from others on the issue, data about the impact of their arrogance is too thin, time is too short, or whatever. The upshot is that it is not likely that you can influence the arrogant behavior, even if the cumulative continuing costs to your job performance are high. In these circumstances, the best approach probably is to keep your distance as much as possible, withdrawing to the bare minimum of required contact. This is a way of coping with the problem, although it is limited in terms of having any kind of long-term effect. It also may continue to be a restriction on your own effectiveness that will hamper you until a more active solution is found.

If you don't have or can't build a climate that discourages arrogant leadership behavior, it raises the question of why you are there. Is it actually a good fit to stay in an environment that blocks both achievement and personal growth? Or are you hanging on due to a fear of the unknown or from inertia? When considering the costs of this restrictive relationship over time, you may have to accept the fact that there is little likelihood of change. It may just be a bad match, and therefore time to move on with your life as you would prefer to live it.

It's certainly not necessarily easy, but the ultimate choice that we all have is whether to stay in a situation that is toxic for us and unlikely to improve much going forward. Consider the re-evaluation in the following example:

> [In the late 90's], Ameet Shah, 24, was successfully laying the groundwork for life as a corporate titan. After graduating from Duke University, he had landed a $50,000-a-year job in New York at J. P. Morgan Chase, working 100-hour weeks on deals

involving companies like Enron and Kmart. But no sooner had Mr. Shah settled into the perks of his new career — expense accounts, car services and enough cash to support an apartment in a doorman building — than his world was shaken by a market downturn and a stream of stories about corporate malfeasance. The deals — and the perks — dried up, many of his colleagues were fired, and Mr. Shah got a peek at capitalism's dark side.

"I saw people who put 15 years of service into the company get laid off in a day because of the irresponsible behavior of corporate executives," he said. "I started thinking that I didn't want to be associated with that." Mr. Shah's disillusionment eventually became so complete that in June — sometime between the indictment of L. Dennis Kozlowski, the chairman of Tyco, for tax fraud and the news that WorldCom had improperly accounted for $3.8 billion in expenses — he quit J. P. Morgan Chase and joined Teach for America. He now lives in a dorm room and teaches summer school in a classroom without air-conditioning in the South Bronx, training to earn $35,000 a year. [31]

In summary, we have been considering some of the most useful factors for deciding how and when to deal with a leader's pattern of arrogant behavior. The three main requirements are to be clear on your goals (get even, effect change, mediate for someone else, balance the situation, etc.), to be clear on the role you're in and the leverage (or lack thereof) that it provides, and to assess the immediate situation and how crucial it is to get beyond a "one person knows it all" approach. And, as our last example suggests, there is always the fourth question: do I want to continue in this relationship under these constraints? None of these are easy questions with easy answers, but having a conscious process will open up more positive avenues than knee-jerk reactions, no matter how satisfying it might be to tell your boss where to go.

CHAPTER 7

Antidotes to Arrogance

We have looked at dealing with arrogance from the standpoint of coping with the arrogance we see in others' behavior. Now let's consider the other half of the problem: handling our *own* tendencies toward arrogant behavior and the consequences that they may have. Coping with others' arrogant behavior is one thing, but dealing with it within ourselves is quite another. When it is you yourself, there is no option to walk away from the relationship or minimize contact. The cumulative costs are highest for ourselves rather than the people who have trouble dealing with us, including:

- Alienating people we need to work with (see coping mechanisms discussed in Chapter 6);
- Being solely dependent on ourselves for right answers and good choices of action;
- Not learning from experience about how well our own ideas fit with others';
- Not learning new things—showing little curiosity about the world;

- Not leaving ourselves open for unexpected and unpredictable ideas and events.

If you believe that you suffer from any one or more of the causes we have identified, you might think about how you can deal with it. The authors of *The Trusted Advisor* state that a key antidote is the ability to create trust with others [32]. They say that trust is based on four factors: credibility, reliability, intimacy and self-orientation. "Trust has multiple dimensions. I might trust your expertise, but distrust (profoundly) your motives (i.e, self-orientation). I might trust your brilliance, but dislike your style of dealing with me (your intimacy)...Winning trust requires that you do well on all four dimensions.

"Most professionals, when asked to talk about trust, instinctively focus on credibility and reliability." Here is how they describe relationships characterized by arrogance as opposed to trusting relationships:

Poor Marks on:	Get Characterized as:
Credibility	Windbags
Reliability	Irresponsible
Intimacy	Technicians
Self-orientation	Devious

The key is to develop an ability to look at oneself as clearly and objectively as possible and to find ways to get honest feedback on how you are coming across to others. Having done that, let's assume that you really are interested in dealing with your own tendencies toward arrogance, and explore some basic approaches that can help. First, we have a simple little test that may help you get started.

WHAT'S MY AQ?
(ARROGANCE QUOTIENT)

Please answer the following 20 questions as True or False

(CIRCLE ONE)

1. Most people around me don't seem to be able to think clearly about things.   T   F

2. If I want things done right, I have to do them myself.   T   F

3. I have to be careful not to spend too much time with the people who are "dead wood" around here.   T   F

4. I can't remember ever saying "I was wrong about that..."   T   F

5. I sometimes amaze even myself with my creativity.   T   F

6. I seem to be a much harder worker than most of the people in my organization.   T   F

7. Most of the people around me don't have the judgment necessary to make big decisions.   T   F

8. I can't remember having ever thought to myself "That was a good point she made..."   T   F

9. I appreciate the fact that people don't argue with me when I know I'm right and they're wrong.   T   F

10. People depend on me almost all the time for guidance.   T   F

11. I really appreciate it when I come into contact with someone who is as smart as I am.   T   F

12. I'm suspicious when I come into contact with someone who thinks they are as smart as I am.   T   F

13. If it weren't for me, this place would fall apart in no time.   T   F

14. I often have to waste too much time helping people catch up with my reasoning processes.   T F

15. I sometimes (briefly) forget how smart I am....   T F

16. It's not worth getting other peoples' ideas on most of the problems I face.   T F

17. I hate being contradicted by people who ought to know better.   T F

18. Thinking clearly seems to be a lost art.   T F

19. It's a waste of time arguing with subordinates since they can't have informed opinions.   T F

20. I could have designed a much better test than this one.   T F

SCORING YOURSELF
Total up the number of True choices. If they total...

5-9 :   You're fairly confident.

10-14 : You'll be described by others as "overbearing" (but not to your face).

15+ :   There's probably no one around to describe you as anything.

1-4 :   You're only fooling yourself!

Now that you have your results, let's look at some practical approaches that we believe may be helpful.

Learning from Past Experiences

A natural first step is to get data about the issue from those likely to have it. The simplest (but not necessarily most comfortable) way to do this is to seek feedback from people with whom you work day-to-day. How do they see your behavioral style? Are you open to ideas or points of view other than your own? Do you punish, in subtle (or not so subtle) ways, subordinates who disagree with you about facts or your predictions of consequences? What do they see as the costs and benefits of your style of collaboration, and, on balance, is it positive in their view? It helps to ask for specific examples, although it may take a while to tease them from the people you are asking. The stronger your tendencies toward arrogance, the more cautious people will be about openly sharing their perceptions with you, since the very act of soliciting their opinions is out of character and likely to make them nervous.

A more formal and systematic way of gathering information about how others see you and your behavior is to have someone conduct a 360° review similar to what was suggested for others in the previous chapter. This mechanism allows those above you, at your own level, and below you to provide feedback in an anonymous format. These kinds of reviews can provide you with valuable information about how you are seen throughout the organization, and if you are acting in an arrogant way, feedback about it is likely to be pretty blunt.

Collecting data is not enough by itself—you obviously must do something with the information. A useful step is to review your own patterns of behavior in situations with others where there is sharing of information, influencing of one another, and the like. It helps to focus on key instances in which others' have described you as being overbearing or closed to any ideas other than your own. Is there a pattern to these occurrences, in timing, in situations, with certain individuals, with types of people, with levels of risk, and so on? In other words, are there consistent triggering events or people? The point is to recognize such patterns and make conscious choices as opposed to automatic arrogant responses that don't serve any useful purpose except to protect your own feelings of superiority or your avoidance of feelings of inferiority.

Using the Past in the Present

If you are discovering some consistent patterns of arrogant behavior and the resulting cost in terms of lost collaboration, it would be useful to engage in some sort of therapeutic process to help you understand more about the sources of your arrogant behavior and what triggers it. Does it manifest itself as a need to be right, to immediately know all the answers (without inquiry), to be the smartest person, etc.? Many times, arrogant behavior is rooted in some inherent insecurity. The therapeutic process can help you identify the sources of such insecurities and test their validity against the realities of your current situation, stage of life and development. A lot of old "fail-safe systems" can be laid to rest simply by getting such assumptions into the open and testing them for continuing relevance. An independent coach, counselor or therapist can provide a safe environment for you to explore the roots of the behavior that is troubling others and perhaps troubling you as well.

Of course, this step is also not as easy to act on as it is to write about. It requires some uncharacteristic behavior, namely owning up to the possibility that your unswervingly confident style may be driven in part by an inability to accept the fact that there are times when you do not know all the answers. If you continue to feel that the only reason you are so confident is that you actually are smarter than everyone around you, then the chances of meaningful exploration of your old hidden assumptions are quite low. A suspension of judgment (especially about yourself) is a prerequisite here, just as it is in many situations that require new perspectives in order to foster new ideas and action options.

Using the Present

Another possibility is that there are important aspects of your current situation that are producing particularly arrogant responses from you. Does your job/career situation present dangers that put a high price on being perceived always as "right" by yourself or those who can influence your career? Are there pressures in your home or family that feel like they require a similar role of infallibility on your part? Are your social patterns tending to put you into competitive situations where you always feel that you have to perform and demonstrate your superior competence?

These kinds of situations can generate the need to demonstrate that you are OK, thereby triggering arrogant behaviors that don't allow others' ideas or opinions to be heard. If you see this pattern as descriptive of you, then the next step is to work on changing the structures you are in: job, social grouping, roles in your family, or some combination of all three. In many instances, radical changes are not required so much as a redefinition of expectations to create a more flexible situation in which you can be more yourself without paying a high price for it. In fact, these situations may trap you into perpetuating the behavior that others see as arrogant and that may not be helpful even though they have become habitual.

You can pay attention to current situations to recognize the signals that are indicators of when you have clicked into "automatic pilot" mode and are not open to influence or are pain in the neck to those around you. The most useful signals usually are internal feelings about an issue. They could be feelings of condescension or they could be feelings of anger at the fact that others would even suggest another interpretation or alternative. It also could be impatience with others' obvious stupidity or self-righteousness (my motives are pure, others' are not). Boredom (I know all this and have done it all—just shut up and get out of my way), is another signal. This is not to suggest that you would never be right; it's just that feelings of dismissal of even the possibility that others have something to contribute are signals that you have closed down.

The result is usually another signal you can use such as observable behaviors that tend to alienate the people with whom you are supposed to be collaborating. Additionally, not listening to what they are saying, shouting them down, ridiculing their ideas or approaches or dismissing them as having no worthwhile opinions on the topic are clear indications that you are not open to others' opinions. When you proceed on your own without regard for others' views, and use evaluative labels on the other people (immature, unsophisticated, naive) as a way of discrediting them without dealing with the actual content of their ideas, it demeans them and prevents good communication.

If you see yourself behaving in these ways, it is important to ask yourself whether this is what you want to have happen. Will this behavior get the short-term results you want? Will it contribute to the kind of longer-term working relationships you want to maintain? If the answer to these questions is no, you can use this a check on yourself. You can step back, let go, and see what happens. This is easiest to do when the stakes are not very high. If things don't go "perfectly" (i.e., not your way), it's not likely to be a disaster. In practice, you will also find out whether the outcome was negative at all. The results will be surprising, at least some percentage of the time. It is also very interesting when the stakes are extremely high. In these instances, stepping back may make the most difference, even if it simply allows the possibility that some refinement or addition will improve the analysis and action chosen. The scope of impact would be much higher in this case.

Having a Process Plan

If you want to be able to behave with a greater behavioral repertoire than simple reflexive arrogance, one of the most powerful aids is to have a plan. By this, we mean a regular process that you try to follow in work situations to gather data, discuss this data with others, analyze patterns, and make decisions about courses of action. You have to follow this plan even when you feel certain that your point of view is superior and you know what should be done. The times when it feels least necessary to do are the times when it can be most helpful. The more certain you feel in advance, the more difference it makes to have a process (similar to the value of due process in a legal court of law for unpopular, and perceived as obviously guilty defendants) to act as a check on your certainty. Following the plan doesn't take much time when your ideas are good and others agree. It does take more time (as it should) when there are legitimate questions and other points of view that will improve the analysis and resulting choices. This process can be relatively simple, consisting of a checklist of questions to be considered, such as:

- Is there a clear problem statement? If not, how can it be clearer?
- Do we have the relevant data? Is there agreement about it?
- Are there conclusions we can reach? How much agreement is there?
- What is our degree of certainty? Do we need more information?
- What are our options, and what criteria do we use to choose among alternatives?
- Are we agreed about the criteria?
- What are we going to do, and who will do it by when?

The process requires everyone to be honest in their responses to you. The steps may be quick, but don't skip some on the assumption that you already know the answer, or you're right back into the arrogant mode that you're trying to minimize.

Personal Role Management

Another approach to minimizing your own tendencies toward arrogant behavior is to make explicit choices about the roles you accept so that arrogance is obviously an inappropriate and ineffective response. An example is to seek out a learning role in a new setting or skill area—stretching yourself to learn in areas where you are untrained. Computer skills fill the bill for many executive techno-phobes. This can be a truly humbling experience, but you have to be willing to make a commitment to stay in the process, taking it a step at a time, even though it feels uncomfortable and beneath you. Your adoption of an arrogant style is exactly what makes this process so hard, since small steps don't lend themselves to projecting an air of competence and mastery. It's like learning to ski as an adult, feeling awkward and foolish while 6-year-olds whiz past you on the beginners' slope.

It is a reasonable rule of thumb that you should set out to learn something truly new every two or three years. It's useful in its own right, and it keeps you aware that the world is a lot larger than the small corner of it that you have mastered. Wide reading on a regular basis can achieve some of this, but it doesn't necessarily challenge the arrogance reflex. Potentially, you can be even more arrogant because you read widely, believing that you are more up to date than anyone else. You need to extend the experience to trying to master something at which you are not already good.

Another useful role structure is to put yourself into situations where you are definitely not in charge or the highest-ranking. It is very instructive to try to influence people who are not deferring to your positional authority. The content of your ideas (and the way you present them) must then carry the weight of argument without the overlay of the "divine right of bosses" to define reality for subordinates. A very instructive model for this process is John Coleman, the former president of Haverford College. His wonderful book, *Blue Collar Journal*[33], describes his experiences (and learning about himself) when he took a leave of absence from leading the college to work in some menial, very un-presidential jobs such as ditch-digging and trash-collecting.

If you're not ready for such an extreme experiment, seeking some kinds of non-leadership roles could be accomplished by being active in community organizations or other non-business institutions, especially if you are top-dog in your own firm. We also have occasionally seen it work while staying within one's own organization. In one highly regarded technical consulting firm, the chairman was sometimes a member of a consulting team headed by a project leader several layers below the chairman in the administrative hierarchy. Their way of doing business focused on doing the best job for the client as being paramount, so deferring to the chairman's weaker ideas was not an acceptable pattern. This gave him a very useful check on his tendency to see himself as the one in the firm with the ultimate grasp of truth and wisdom. Admittedly, his ideas were not dismissed out of hand (he had no trouble getting heard in team meetings), but neither were they accepted when they were technically inferior to others' contributions.

Both of these approaches—learning really new skills and putting yourself in non-leadership positions with more modest role expectations—require a conscious choice to get out of your comfort zone; structuring situations for yourself that are not necessarily comfortable but have broader payoffs. The main payoff is, in fact, to reduce the need to maintain protective comfort by always being the smartest, most correct person so there is no uncertainty about how good you are and how well you're doing. Maintaining the stance that you are always number one (and must be) reduces ambiguity but can be a major impediment to making a contribution in tough situations. It is better to practice letting go of comfort than to expect to be able to do it in some very high-stakes crisis.

Cultivating a Truth-Teller

There is a strategy for coping with one's own arrogant tendencies that is several thousand years old. This is to make sure that someone in your immediate circle of friends, family and colleagues is a "truth-teller" for you; that is, a confidante that you can be completely yourself with and whom you trust to tell you what they really think, no matter how well it matches up with your own views. They are not over-awed by you, nor do they feel that their livelihood depends on remaining in your good graces. The relationship is one of true honesty and commitment to one another over the long haul.

In order to have this type of relationship, you are required to be honest as well. A one-way process has no staying power, and without you priming the pump, it will soon become another ritualized relationship that is comfortable but not of much real value. There can be lots of "yes men" (really yes persons) in the entourage, but one truth-teller can provide considerable balance. Without this input, arrogant executives have a tendency to become more and more legends in their own minds, and be less and less able to remove their own auras as a source of obscuring noise in difficult situations.

One way to have a truth-teller available is to hire an organizational consultant or executive coach to work with you. This person can gather information about your leadership style from others and then have conversations with you to identify ways that you could lead more effectively. Here again, the probability of success from working with a coach or consultant is completely dependent on having a trusting relationship with that person and on your willingness to be completely open and listen to ideas that are likely to be somewhat painful.

Being Curious

It will sound like a bit of a truism, but one way to get yourself out of only seeing what you already know is to actually be interested in doing it. It is very helpful to have a real sense of curiosity about what's going on, how things work, what's changing, how other people see the world, and the like. This is a stance that tends to reward itself, since the process of real discovery usually leads to feeling glad that you asked the question, which in turn makes it more likely that you'll be curious next time. Although there are clearly differences in peoples' predispositions toward curiosity, this is something that can be enhanced with practice.

The Corner Office, a recent book by *New York Times* business columnist Adam Bryant, summarizes five common themes about lessons learned by the many CEO's he has interviewed for his column.[34] To our point here, one of the five is what he calls *Passionate Curiosity*. His leaders acknowledge that they are usually expected to show a public face which projects certainty and decisiveness. But they add that whenever possible, they must also be seeking out new information, listening to what others' think and feel and testing whether current practices are as effective as they could or should be. They describe themselves as both needing to learn all the time and enjoying the learning process. This is about as big a contrast as you could get with leaders who behave as if they have absolutely nothing useful to learn.

Sense of Humor

Finally, one of the best antidotes for the metamorphosis from competence to arrogance may simply be a good sense of humor:

the ability or tendency to be tickled with absurdities, odd combinations, surprises, and the like. Many of these instances arise in relation to oneself, through doing things which in hindsight may look pretty silly. Arrogant people can't accept their own ability to do silly things, or see themselves as the butt of a joke. They tend to take themselves so seriously that they require that others do the same, or they take the lack of seriousness as a sign of disrespect.

The arrogant executive may be witty, and able to put others down with caustic remarks that can draw laughs, but they don't tend to laugh at themselves, which is the essence of being able to laugh in general. A non-arrogant viewpoint of the world is required in order to recognize and accept contradictions, mismatches, and instinctual responses that turn out to be the opposite of what was needed. Possibly a good sense of humor simply means accepting fallibility as a natural, even valued part of the human condition—one that makes things more interesting rather than just sloppy.

CHAPTER 8

Institutional Arrogance

We now want to consider arrogance at a different level, tied to whole groups or organizations rather than simply as residing in selected individuals. What we're talking about is a pattern of arrogant behavior in the processes of the organization, almost a basic way of life for members. This pattern shows up in several arenas:

- The organizational climate within the system (how members deal with each other day to day);
- The way members of the organization deal with people outside the system;
- The stances taken by the organization's leaders in highly visible actions, events or decisions that are interpreted by the public as representing the identity and basic philosophy of the organization;
- The consequences of being in first place in a new 'hot' market.

We will examine each of these in turn.

Climate within the Organization

There are some organizations whose pervasive climate, or feel, is one of arrogant behavior as a basic style of operating. People basically play a game where points are scored by treating others as inferior, incapable, or unwilling to extend the kinds of effort that is needed in order to be a true team player. A typical driver of such a process is the norm that people should "sound positive" about everything. Uncertainty is not all right, and being undecided is considered being weak or wishy-washy. The true contributor always knows what's next and best to do, no matter what the conditions. Since conditions don't always neatly produce this certainty in anyone, the norm actually says you must appear certain no matter what, leading to a good deal of posturing and overstatement about what will happen if a certain course of action is chosen. A typical accompanying pattern is people cutting each other up in an attempt to win arguments, and the resulting climate tends to be relatively harsh and unforgiving. Ridiculing others' ideas is encouraged as a means of demonstrating one's prowess and scoring points with peers or superiors.[35]

Arrogant climates generate their own rhetoric—the sayings and myths that maintain the expected attitude of superiority even though individual members may come and go. One of the most common themes is "We're all the best here," or its corollary, "We only hire the very best people." We had a client whose members described proudly how the company only hired from the top one percent of the best schools, even though as a single criterion, it left something to be desired as a predictor of success within the business. Some of the actual best contributors didn't fit this hiring pattern at all, but the myth remained unchallenged.

In the high-arrogance organizational climate, public internal meetings, such as progress updates, usually feature executives telling the troops how smart everyone is and how dumb the competitors' people are; anyone who thinks otherwise is negative or disloyal. It is obviously very hard to honestly and accurately assess what you're up against in such a climate. Although people do get together in private to try to assess reality, the tone from the bigger events can hover like a cloud and make it feel risky to raise questions about challenges and what's really likely to happen. There is usually a vague sense that you could be reported to higher-ups as unreliable or unsound, much like neighbors informed on one another during the Stalinist era in the USSR or people in the entertainment industry were pressured to denounce one another as Communists during the McCarthy era.

This climate also tends to feel quite competitive. Status points are believed to be conferred on those who can consistently win their arguments by beating down or dismissing others' ideas as naive or misguided. Arrogant behavior is admired and rewarded as a means of scoring points and getting attention, not to mention getting one's way in choosing courses of action. One company we know tried to get their sales force to put increased attention toward a new product area and devised a commission plan to make doing so attractive to sales people. When the scheme was presented to the president, he asked if it were possible that a sales person could earn more than he (the president himself) would earn under the proposed plan. He was told that it was theoretically possible if a sales person were to sell ten times as much as the rest of the sales force combined. The president then disapproved implementation of the plan!

Besides gaining informal stature, people believe that arrogance is formally rewarded by the system as well. Promotions appear to come more readily to those who practice effective arrogance as a management style. People often claim credit for what their subordinates did, and in a high-arrogance climate, this is not rejected as underhanded, it is simply considered part of being a smart manager. From reading press reports and talking with former employees, it appears that Kodak's lack of success in the 80's and 90's—as they tried to diversify to prevent the fall-off of film-based pictures (as digital cameras and video took market share as had been predicted for nearly 20 years)—was due to executive arrogance. They felt that they could run businesses where they didn't really understand the dynamics of the market. (To be more precise, they appeared to believe that there were no businesses that they did not understand.) The same phenomenon caused Exxon to lose over $600 million dollars after their failed experiment into various aspects of Exxon Enterprises, their foray into the computer business..

Leaders Set the Tone

When a group of people is trying to arrive at some consensual view of "truth" in a meeting, the formal company hierarchy is often used as the key factor in sorting out "facts" from fictions. The highest-ranking person gets to define reality, and the others are expected to defer to them whether they have the appropriate experiences/knowledge or not. The senior person may have been out of the front-line action for many years and yet be allowed to tell everyone else "what it's really like out there."

As we discussed in the chapter on symbols, the system's workplace facilities are used to reinforce the climate of arrogance. Major emphasis is placed on using office size and furnishings as indicators of status; there are dress code norms about how people should look at different levels to help maintain appropriate distances between the levels, and a norm which says people who don't dress right should be ignored as having little of value to contribute. This is reinforced even more strongly by separate facilities such as executive dining rooms, reserved (nearby) parking spaces and exclusive washrooms so serious people will not be distracted by contact with less important beings. Perks are seen as major motivators (which they are, if members buy into the arrogance climate) and people are encouraged to take advantage of them and "flaunt it if you've got it." The receivers of such bounty are truly amazed when they are told that others in the organization are not universally pleased with their hold on a disparate portion of the system's resources.

Enron's stock price, which hit a high of $90 per share in mid-2000, caused shareholders to lose nearly $11 billion when it plummeted to less than a $1 by the end of November 2001. During this time, the leaders of Enron (Kenneth Lay and Jeffrey Skilling) were exhorting people to buy Enron stock while selling their own positions.[36] Similarly, during 2006 and 2007 as investor losses mounted, Bear Stearns actually increased its exposure in the risky mortgage-backed assets that were central to the subprime mortgage crisis. Its leaders, Alan D. Schwartz and Sam Molinaro, pushed forward despite warning signs that were given to them by key subordinates. Similarly, Lehman Brothers collapsed at the same time that CEO Richard Fuld kept assuring its lenders that the firm's financial situation was very strong.

> "If only Chairman Fuld had kept his ear close to the ground on the inner workings of his firm—both its triumphs and its mistakes. If he had listened to his generals, met people who formed the heart and soul of Lehman Brothers, the catastrophe might have been avoided. But instead of this, he secluded himself in his

palatial offices up there on the thirty-first floor, remote from the action, dreaming only of accelerating growth, nursing ambitions far removed from reality." [37]

To be sure, a tone of leadership arrogance is not inevitable:

"Tim White (then publisher of the *Albany Times Union*, later of the *San Francisco Examiner*) ran an offsite meeting of his management team of a dozen people. Throughout this meeting, Tim conveyed a sense of technical mastery, calm, and wisdom. Yet he did so by hardly ever expressing an opinion, making a technical point, or articulating a decision. Instead, almost all of his input consisted of visually and verbally scanning the table, seeking emotional expressions on the faces of his team…The meeting was highly successful. Not only were decisions made, but everyone felt involved and consulted and that the process was "fair." Tim did not lack for technical competence, and he had strong opinions, but he achieved most of his ends by devoting his attention almost entirely to observing, understanding, and articulating the needs of others. He achieved high-content results almost entirely through low-content leadership." [38]

The other interesting arena for internal arrogance is intergroup collaboration and general relations. Even when there is not a system-wide climate encouraging arrogance, there are often sub-groups that develop it as a style for dealing with other groups in the organization who are perceived to be not like themselves. In technical companies, scientists or engineers can develop a self-congratulatory view of their own importance in relation to the non-technical members whom they see as simply being carried along for the ride. The people on the "creative" side in advertising agencies often dismiss account management people as necessary evils, and vice-versa. People performing roles where they touch the product last, such as sales people in a consumer products company, often refer to themselves as the "real money makers" and all the rest as "burden," as if there would be anything for them to be selling without everyone doing their part in the total process.

Some organizations have class distinctions based on educational level. We have worked for several pharmaceutical research organizations, and in every one of them there has been a clear break between the Ph.D.s and all others. Sometimes this schism is so big that nearly no communication can cross it, and valuable information is kept from both groups. The assumption by Ph.D.s that they have nothing to learn from those without the Ph.D. and therefore shouldn't have to deal with them often closes off an important source of information (the ideas, views, experiences of the non-Ph.D. population) to say nothing of impeding cross-functional teamwork in the organization.

Team cohesiveness that is usually a desirable thing can go too far and become team arrogance. One of the unanticipated consequences of strong cohesiveness is that walls get built around the team and it becomes difficult for information to flow into or out of the team. Cooperation with other groups gets more difficult as a result. One of our clients has three cohesive software development teams working for the same vice president. Each team is responsible for bringing a new product to market. In a typical sequence, one team adds some features to their product that the vice president thinks would be good to have included in another team's product. He suggests to the second team that they add the features that the first team had invented. When the second team goes to the first team to learn more about the features and how they work in that team's application, the first team essentially refuses to give the relevant information to the second team. Their attitude is one of disdain for the members of the second team rather than one of cooperation and sharing.

Here's another example from the product development area. A small company created a very good software product and licensed it to a much larger software company. The large company eventually bought the small development company. The employees of the small company were told by their leader not to have any more than 10 minutes of interaction with large company people in any given day—50 minutes per week—because he was trying to protect them from being "polluted" by the large company's people who he saw as much less bright than his own people. The small company culture and behavior underlined those differences. They had entrances to their area of the building controlled by badge cards that denied access to parent company people. The physical exclusion was to emphasize the separation of cultures and emphasize the negative value they put on mixing the two.

The point is that a climate of arrogance within a sub-group breeds barriers and a tendency to dismiss what others know or think about almost anything, including those things about which they have the best experience. This is a process that kills free information flow in an organization and makes it very hard to spot problems before they have become big enough to be crises.

We're hot and you're not!

There is also a form of group or institutional arrogance that gives members an inflated sense of their importance just because they are members of the group or institution. We have worked with companies that have enjoyed rapid growth and great success in the marketplace. In some cases, the success bred a form of institutional arrogance. Digital Equipment Corporation in the 70's and early 80's was such a place. DEC dominated the minicomputer market, and many of their employees were young, bright and apt to believe that they and the company were invincible. Tom Peters' 1983 book, *In Search of Excellence* identified DEC as one of the role models of excellence. Many of those in the company became even more certain that they could do no wrong. Ten years later, it was a very different story in a vastly changed competitive landscape. Having held onto their particular paradigm even as it was becoming less and less relevant to emerging corporate and personal computing patterns, they shrank and then were absorbed by Compaq. Was that kind of institutional arrogance one of the reasons that DEC was not able to adapt to the vast changes occurring in the marketplace? Were DEC's leaders so sure of themselves based on their past success that they felt they didn't need to listen to those inside or outside the company who were sending out warning signals? [39]

Other companies that were "hot" some years ago and came to believe their own hype have had a sad awakening in the recent past as the market landscape changed in ways they couldn't or didn't anticipate. In the computer field, there were those who didn't see DOS as the replacement for CPM (Anyone remember Osborne?;Visicalc?). There were those who didn't see minicomputers as largely replacing mainframe computers. Remember when IBM ruled the field? Today, Microsoft has a market valuation considerably higher than that of IBM and Apple has a valuation higher than either of them. There were those who didn't see the revolution created by client / server networks and distributed relational databases running on them, to say nothing of the revolution in cell phones, personal information managers, notebook computers and tablets.

Today, everyone knows that you can't count on things staying the same for long. Every year, there are revolutions in hardware and software that are in the process of dramatically changing the way all forms of information are assembled, stored, disseminated and used. In fact, the dividing lines between film, video, television, telephone and internet connections are blurring. None of the companies in those industries can afford institutional arrogance, and the ones that stay around long enough to be recognized, are not in danger of becoming obsolete.

Patterns of Outside Contacts

An internal climate of arrogance will very likely carry over into influencing the way members of the organization deal with the outside world. If arrogant behavior is a basic ingredient in how people deal with one another internally, it is very hard to turn it off when dealing with outsiders. If anything, the urge may be even stronger since the other person is assumed to not be one of the elite, that is, not one of us—"the best and the brightest."

The most visible and damaging manifestation of this tendency occurs when dealing with customers. The many recent books dealing with providing high quality service to customers are full of examples of how not to do it, and many of them have a common theme: assuming an arrogant stance toward the customer and thereby turning them off even when you have great products. This stance can take many forms:

- We are the professionals, so you should take the process or product we will design and not worry about it;
- You can't possibly understand the complexities of our business, so just try fit your requests to our schedule (we'll tell you how and when);
- The features in this product are what you *should* want,

in contrast with the un-sophisticated expectations you now have;
- This is what we have/do; if you don't like it, go somewhere else.

We are not saying that most organizations' representatives take this approach with their customers, but there are plenty of examples. One of the most famous, of course, is the quote attributed to the chairman of General Motors, "What's good for GM is good for the country." In its time, this attitude was used to justify almost any decision top management wanted to make, no matter how negative the apparent impact on employees or the public at large. In its glory days, IBM's people had a reputation for sending a clear message about how bright and professional they were and how they would be happy to help bring their naive customers up to speed.

Apple, which was such an important pioneer in the development of the personal computer, saw its market share plunge because of its arrogance in being unwilling to open its operating system to other manufacturers and to outside software developers for many years. Apple declared itself outside the mainstream, which is where it remains today in terms of their percentage of personal computers, though that is changing with the move to a Unix-based operating system and dual-core computers. (They have also made hay with many other innovative devices,). One of the reasons that each of those companies suffered in the marketplace is that they were not tuned into what was happening. They felt they knew more than others and therefore had no need to listen to the views of customers or other "outsiders". It is easy to ignore what is going on outside when the primary focus is on internal organizational genius and crediting others' ideas may threaten the shared assumptions that maintain this identity.

Another indicator of arrogance carryover is the feeling customers get that service is being provided very grudgingly, if at all. There is usually an implicit attitude on the part of company representatives that the problems could not have been caused by their (perfect) products, so they must stem from some sort of user error. The prototype of this pattern was undoubtedly the automaker Audi's response when drivers experienced sudden (and very dangerous) unexpected acceleration with automatic transmission in Audi sedans: "there can't be anything wrong with the car, so it must be due to driver error." Very serious accidents were dismissed as the victims' fault, as if for some mysterious reason Audi drivers were dumber or more error-prone than those who drove Hondas or Fords. More recently, Steve Jobs told early iPhone users that their reception problems were caused by the way they were holding their phones.

In 2010, Toyota engaged in similar behavior in response to a similar problem with unexpected acceleration in their cars:

> "Strategists expressed amazement that a company with Toyota's reputation advantages repeatedly dismissed reports of problems, communicated mainly through press releases—which underscored a fortress-like position—and then begrudgingly confirmed bits of evidence, ensuring that the story would play out in damaging increments.
>
> 'Toyota blew it,' says Brad Burns, who ran communications at WorldCom, the telecommunications giant leveled by a 2001 accounting scandal. 'It's been the proverbial death by a thousand cuts. They knew they had problems long ago, whether it was a mechanical issue or operator error, but they knew they had an issue they had to deal with. And rather than put public safety over profits, they appear to have listened to the product liability lawyers and they totally lost it. It's brand damage.' " [40]

The problem is not limited to car manufacturers. A similar pattern was evident when Intel tried to dismiss the documented findings of a university professor who found that their Pentium chip could cause calculation errors. Only after IBM publicly announced that the incidence of errors was far greater than Intel had said they were did Intel begin to admit they had a problem. Without IBM's clout, individual Pentium owners would have been stonewalled in the same way Audi and Toyota owners were—by being told that the problem was in their use of the product and not with the product itself.

As companies work to save money, a new example of perceived institutional arrogance has emerged. Many companies increasingly are turning to the use of "auto attendant" telephone systems, where a computer voice guides the customer through a range of options and sometimes attempts to resolve things directly. Customers increasingly have to go through a number of choices before being able to talk with a real person, and even then, it is increasingly likely that the person will be someone working in an outsourced call center in India. Paul English, a Boston-based consumer advocate and entrepreneur,r was so frustrated by his customer service experiences that he began a website that ranked companies in terms of how difficult it is to get through to a knowledgeable customer service person. The website now is operated by volunteers who share stories and ratings of more than 1,500 companies, and it has a very interesting video (www.gethuman.com) [41]

At a more general level, an arrogant climate encourages members to ignore recurring problems, especially when reported by outsiders, whether customers or government agencies. As a result, an organization with an arrogant climate tends to delay the collection of significant feedback and delays or dismisses paying serious attention to patterns where something meaningful could be learned and applied to current operations.

Relations with outside suppliers tend to take a similar pattern. They are made to jump through hoops in order to prove that they are "worthy" of being dealt with, not just about relevant criteria such as price, quality and schedule, but also about style, form, and showing the proper deference to arrogant contacts from the company. The expectation is that the suppliers will show that they're OK—a somewhat degrading process that can slop over into being illegal as well.

If a company has dealers or other middlemen, they can also come in for their share of grief from an arrogant climate. They get little consideration when meetings, rollouts and other events are scheduled, on the assumption that it is their problem to keep up anyway, so why coddle them? They tend to get little support for their efforts, and they will be blamed when products don't move at the expected pace. Again, there is a lack of listening to their problems and what they are learning about the products' strengths and weaknesses in the marketplace. In a truly arrogant climate, one's products are always assumed to have no weaknesses to learn about anyway.

All of the effects we are talking about here show up particularly clearly in those industries where, because of the nature of the work, the typical organization historically has had no competition. They have been able to do their business in a very dictatorial manner, establishing the rules and the expectations for what service should be and what it should cost (with government regulatory agencies providing the only structural check, if any, on this approach). They tend to develop procedures for their own convenience rather than as responses to customer problems. IBM's minions could get away with their condescending behavior toward customers when they were the only well-established game in town, but in today's world of multiple choices about how to acquire computing power it's a show that doesn't play very well. To their credit, IBM has developed a very different public face emphasizing their desire and ability to solve complex problems for their customers and be a true partner with the customer.

To take another prime example, for many years American telephone companies generally held monopolies over their particular territories, and customers had to deal with them as the only available option. With the ever-increasing presence of cable companies, cell phones and VOIP (voice over internet protocol) telephone service, traditional phone companies have long been scrambling to shift cultures where arrogance was enshrined in the old joke's phrase, "We don't have to—we're the phone company..." (in Lily Tomlin's wonderful portrayal of Ernestine, the telephone operator). A similar upheaval has happened in a number of areas due to *deregulation of utilities*. There now are rival sources of power within a geographic region, and a customer can actually make the choice to switch to another provider if they are not satisfied. Again, it generates considerable pressure to change cultures and operating procedures that were based on "we're the only game in town" complacency.

Visible Public Actions

Institutional arrogance is most visible to the outside world through actions taken by a system's leaders during crises or special events. These actions are interpreted by observers as glimpses of the "character" of the organization, as if it were a person.

Peter Goodman's analysis of corporations' management of severe crises provides several very striking examples, such as the BP Gulf Oil Spill in April 2010:

> "Many analysts say the company erred in putting its message in the hands of its CEO, Tony Hayward.... His words of regret were delivered with a British accent, and he complicated his task with a series of tin-eared utterances.... When he apologized to those harmed by the spill... he tacked on two sentences that would overshadow all else. 'There's no one who wants this thing over more than I do,' he said. 'I'd like my life back.' With this, Mr. Hayward opened the gates to Sound-Bite Hell. .... Pundits gleefully pointed out that the life he yearned to reclaim featured millions of dollars in compensation, a point reinforced when he took leave of the disaster to spend time with his family—at a yacht race. Mr. Hayward's travails illustrate another perilous lesson from the crisis-management handbook: Although strategists constantly hector executives to stick with the script, ad-libbed gaffes are common. Some of this is rooted in the culture of CEO-dom. Bosses are accustomed to being obeyed as authorities, making them confident in their abilities to charm and persuade—a trait that can cause trouble when the audience is no longer a room full of underlings but a panel of congressional interrogators or a pack of reporters wielding recording devices." [42]

Mr. Hayward subsequently was relieved of his job but the damage had been done.

To take another example, we have already mentioned the Audi leaders' responses to the sudden acceleration problem. Their actions included stonewalling ("there is no problem; it doesn't really happen"); saying to forget it, they were on top of it (our painstaking investigations are continuing); and blaming the victims (our cars are fine, so it must be that the drivers are at fault). In response, the public said, fine, have it your way—and acted accordingly. The victims sued and potential buyers of new cars said "no way". The market for Audi's automatic transmission sedans evaporated. Their denials smacking of perceived arrogance killed that product line, and almost killed the company as well because people resented the company's expressed attitudes almost as much as they disliked the performance problems of the car itself.

We can also consider General Motors again in this regard. About twelve years ago they instituted a number of major plant closings. Top executives were still paying themselves large and visible bonuses while coping with hard times by closing plants like the one in Flint, Michigan. Public questioning was met with silence or vague responses such as "You couldn't possibly understand the burden and complexity of such decisions." (i.e., buzz off....) This stance was made all the more visible by Michael Moore in his tenacious documentary film "Roger & Me," about his attempts to discuss the Flint closing with Roger Smith, then GM's Chairman and CEO. Most of the film shows the condescending dismissals, ridicule, and rejection he got when trying to contact Smith. Whether or not it's all true, the GM executives came across as arrogant, disinterested, and unwilling to be bothered about the impact of their decisions on the lives of extremely loyal long-term GM employees and their families.

Years before the BP spill in the Gulf, the Exxon Valdez oil spill incident in Alaska represented another highly visible event that called for some kind of public corporate response from oil giant Exxon. The company invested enormous resources to cope with the impact of the accident, but the company leaders tended to say "Just keep out of it—we'll take care of it in our own wise way," instead of working with various groups to solve the problems. It came across as dismissive arrogance and lost them points in the public's perception, even though they were spending large sums of money to try to make things right. We suspect that the frequency of lawsuits against them was increased by the tone of the response in addition to the impact of the triggering event, and all of this was strangely destined to provide no learning and be repeated by BP.

We can contrast these examples to another critical event that could have gone just as badly: the Tylenol tampering incident that resulted in several deaths from tainted capsules. The leaders of the Tylenol manufacturer, Johnson & Johnson, might have followed the lead of Audi or Toyota and said something like "The problem is a madman, our hands are tied, and the odds are that there are no more bad capsules out there (or very few), so stop worrying." Instead they acknowledged that people were worried and could not feel confidence in the existing stocks of Tylenol, so they pulled all of them off the shelves at great cost rather than risk any more lives. They knew they were throwing away mostly good product. In our estimation, this customer sensitive approach saved Tylenol as a valuable long-term product. In fact, Tylenol gained market share in the months following the episode and it continues to be a major product for J&J. Without such a straightforward and bold response, Tylenol would not have sold well at any price, just like the old Audi sedan.

The cases we've cited are also often used in graduate school courses on business ethics, examining a company's responsibility in risky or damaging situations. Our analysis has suggested to us that a lot of corporate ethical issues have the theme of institutional arrogance as a consistent driver. It overlays leaders' decision-making processes and clouds the results. A major consideration is obviously the bottom line—how can we do what will cost us the least or make us the most money—but the arrogance factor acts as an influence on the analysis itself. It can blind leaders to other fall-out costs (loss of market share, reduced public confidence, a corporate image as being rapacious and selfish, etc.) and lead to true sub-optimization. In their arrogant mode, leaders feel that people should either get out of their way or that they'll be too dense to spot what's happening. It's like the arrogance of the politician caught with a hand in the public till assuming they will never be found out (remember the House Post Office scandal or Rep. Jefferson's cash in his freezer?)

While acting as if they can do whatever they choose, events often prove this to be a major miscalculation. Arrogant executives are always at risk of doing something that comes back to haunt them because they believe they are not subject to the constraints and standards applied to ordinary people. In 2012, a perfect example about power and the abuse of power came to light. The Murdoch Scandal was reported by newspapers in England, Australia, Canada and the United States and had television coverage on the BBC and PBS:

> A series of investigative reports by journalists around the globe have put Rupert Murdoch's News Corporation at the center of a new hacking scandal. The allegations could be far more devastating than the scandal that brought an end to the News of the World newspaper last year, since this one strikes at the financial heart of Mr. Murdoch's empire: News Corp's valuable television holdings. [43]
>
> What we see here is a pattern, going back decades, of Rupert Murdoch playing God in British politics. Those he supported achieved power. In power, they helped his business interests....In the end, it is the elaborate, intricate series of connections between the Murdoch papers, the British government and the London police force that is truly mind-boggling.
>
> In an earlier inquiry, Rebecca Brooks admitted that News Corp. had paid off London police for information, including

emails of victims whose phones were then hacked. In the Dowler case, the News of the World hacked the phone of the murdered girl but did not tell her parents she had been killed, reportedly waiting instead to listen to phone messages. [44]

As we have suggested, it is our view this is becoming more prevalent as more powerful worldwide competition becomes a fact of life and nobody can operate for very long in a self-contained arena without constraints. More leaders are recognizing that no matter what their personal estimations of themselves, institutional arrogance and the "closed system" style is a recipe for a dead-end strategy.

Hence the big push for a true customer-focused approach (as if this were ever *not* important), strategic alliances, teaming with suppliers and the like—all aimed at reducing the tendency for the institution's leaders to think of their system as a free-wheeling entity too important to be constrained or challenged.

Organizational Limitations of Institutional Arrogance

To summarize the main themes here, effective organizations of the 21st century must be customer focused, responsive, flexible, lean, productive and quickly adaptable in order to succeed in the global economy. As organizations move toward more participatory forms of management, flatter organization structures, more cross-functional and team-based processes and the like, the negative effects of arrogance in the organization's culture are exaggerated. Teams can't function well if there is arrogance that accentuates differences and declares one sub-group better than others. This tends to be particularly true where organizations have implemented self-managed team structures.

All of these changes (which, at various times, have come under headings like re-engineering, total quality, open book management) are aimed at eliminating sub-group boundaries, awkward hand-offs and "disconnects" between groups in order that employees can have a better sense of the whole system. Smoothing and speeding-up these processes requires the capacity to do very good reality-testing both inside and outside the organization, and a culture of arrogance makes both of these much more difficult. Alienation of external constituents is also quite costly, potentially losing customers and blocking the strategic partnerships that are becoming more and more important for survival in an age of uncertainty.

This alienation can include the public at large that takes its cue from the visible behavioral manifestations of a system's leaders and generalizes to the "personality" of the organization and even to its whole field of endeavor, such as investment banking. To take another example from Goodman's crisis management article:

> "If there was panic and chaos inside Goldman Sachs [in Spring, 2010 during the mortgage meltdown investigation], the company kept it hidden, maintaining a consistent communications posture throughout its brush with unwanted scrutiny: Yield little.
>
> Yet in opting to mount an aggressive defense, the company appears to have intensified criticism. As many communications experts see it, Goldman took a series of unsavory but not crippling disclosures about how it profited before, during and after a global financial crisis and—through a public relations strategy built on arrogance and insensitivity to the national mood—turned itself into a symbol of Wall Street shenanigans." [45]

Finally, an arrogant culture tends to block development of internal talent. The over-emphasis on always appearing to be certain and confident makes it harder to learn from experience.

And, there is a tendency to drive out strong people who recognize the game for what it is, and feel that it's too inhibiting of both performance and learning. It's fairly obvious that losing the people who can be most helpful in fostering quick adaptations to unpredictable events is not a pattern that will guarantee survival in a tough world.

CHAPTER 9

Arrogance in Other Places

For most of this discussion, we have concentrated on arrogant behavior in leaders of organizations, primarily business organizations. We don't mean to imply, however, that arrogance isn't present in many other areas. This chapter will take a brief look at arrogance in a variety of other settings. Wherever dominant executive arrogance occurs, we think its dynamics and consequences tend to be similar. But in settings outside the usual organizational ones, both the dynamics and the consequences can be a lot more dramatic, just because they tend to be a lot more public.

Politics

Throughout human history, the arena of politics is replete with examples of rampant arrogance, all the more so because it is a personal quality that leads people to seek positions which reinforce their high opinions of themselves. For example, consider the arrogance of President Nixon and his people throughout the Watergate affair. They actually thought that they could get away with anything, and when they were first caught, that they could keep it quiet by covering it up. The whole affair also provided an unusually clear view of an underlying assumption that characterized the Nixon administration: the general public is so stupid and uninvolved that its leaders can do anything they want and get away with it.

Henry Kissinger is famous for his arrogance. In spite (or perhaps partly because) of his arrogance, he was enormously successful as Secretary of State. His arrogance often was expressed as extreme self-confidence and absolute certainty that he was right. He also was able to back up his opinions with massive amounts of factual information, much of it carried in his head. Heads of state around the world were impressed with Kissinger's intelligence and knowledge and tended to trust him (or at least his competence) as a consequence. When dealing with those heads of state, his arrogance probably was kept in check by their own stature, which could not be lightly dismissed. His dealings with his State Department staff and others in the U.S. government were another story, however, and subordinates and "peers" usually didn't stand a chance against his unwavering certainty.

The check overdraft scandal of the House Post Office is another example. Many Representatives simply believed that they were exempt from the rules that apply to the rest of us. When they were caught, their explanations (ranging from outright denial to "rank has its privileges") were extraordinarily arrogant.

During President George H.W. Bush's term, his Chief of Staff John H. Sununu was widely reported to be almost pathologically arrogant, demonstrating repeatedly that he believed that everyone was less intelligent than he. When confronted by the press about this, his frequent response was, "Me? I'm a pussycat." Sununu reportedly took personal trips, for skiing and other purposes, and classified them as official. When it was made public that he had commandeered a government jet to visit his dentist in Boston, he defended his "right" to have done so because he was so important and his time was so valuable. Sununu became the subject of much late-night television humor over the incident, including speculation about how top secret government-sponsored super-toilets were being developed to make him really productive....[46] "Delusions of grandeur are Sununu's biggest problem. He craves the challenge of public life but demands the perks of the corporate suite."[47]

In recent years, arrogance in politics has reached new heights. In a 2009 story about the looming financial crisis, the trio of Robert Rubin, Larry Summers and Alan Greenspan showed utter disdain for people who challenged their points of view. Similar arrogant behavior was on display by the trio of Dick Cheney, Donald Rumsfeld and Paul Wolfowitz during George W. Bush's first term with regard to their certainty about weapons of mass destruction in Iraq and the need to start the war. All those who voiced different points of view were summarily dismissed. The sweepstakes seems to have been swept, however, by former House Speaker Newt Gingrich in the Republican primary battles for the 2012 presidential nomination. His disdain for having to be on a debating platform with the mere mortals around him seems to ooze through the television set, and he seems at times almost apologetic that it's such an unfair fight. As Frank Bruni recounted in a NY Times op-ed column titled "Self-adoration Reaches Newt Heights," "Over the years he has directly or indirectly compared himself to Moses, William Wallace (a k a 'Braveheart'...), the Duke of Wellington, Charles de Gaulle, and repeatedly, Ronald Reagan, as when he recently said, 'Because I am much like Reagan and Margaret Thatcher, I'm such an unconventional political figure that you really need to design a unique campaign that fits the way I operate.'"[48]

We could cite example after example from the political arena, where players often get rewarded with more influence when they declare themselves to be the source of wisdom on whatever suits them and the situation. The point is, as the old saying goes, "Power corrupts; absolute power corrupts absolutely". High political or appointive office tends to bring with it a lot of power, perks and publicity. It is hard in such circumstances for people not to begin to believe that they really are better than other people. Yet some politicians manage to hang on to their sense of perspective, humility and humanity in spite of the heady atmosphere in Washington. Presidents Truman, Ford and Carter, Senator George Mitchell and others are examples. When Harry Truman was President, he famously took walks around Washington (his "morning constitutional" he called them), accompanied by some staff members and reporters. He was seen as "everyman" at the time. Similarly, when Jimmy Carter was inaugurated, he chose to forgo the traditional limousine cavalcade and walk between the Capitol and the White House (and subsequently to wear cardigan sweaters and carry his own luggage) to show that he was no different from anyone else. (Barack Obama also walked the inaugural parade route).

These seemingly small gestures were important because they gave people a sense that their leaders shared a common humanity with them. This is a style that also has a long-term impact on relations with colleagues. Senator George Mitchell in his role as Senate President always treated everyone with respect and humility, and probably was chosen to represent the United States in resolving the situation in Northern Ireland and to be our envoy to the Middle East at least in part because of that characteristic. In all of these examples of non-arrogant leader styles, the difference was not a lack of self-regard, since they all certainly felt confidence in their own abilities or they wouldn't have been in their positions. Rather it was the willingness also to listen and be influenced by others at crucial times. Dismissing others out of hand was not essential to maintaining their own sense of competence.

The Arts

Much has been written about all the prima donnas in the art and music world from opera divas to world famous conductors to music stars. Often their fame goes to their heads and they become insufferable people for others to be around. It must be next to impossible to be genuinely better than all others in your chosen field and to keep your sense of perspective as also being just another human being. Vladimir Horowitz was considered to be the world's best pianist for many decades. He also was reputed to be very arrogant in his dealings with others, which he got away with because of his enormous talent. The same has been said about Maria Callas, Kathleen Battle, Arturo Toscanini, George Szell, Pablo Picasso and many others. Friends and colleagues who stayed connected with these people learned to suffer in silence, presumably for the reflected glory of being associated with greatness, or because they were in danger of becoming the target of sudden outbursts of anger triggered by the genius' sense of entitlement.

In the field of architecture, the landscape is littered with designers who are reputed to have had egos even larger than their creations. America's own Frank Lloyd Wright was famous not just for his creativity, but also for his willingness to browbeat his clients and dismiss any differences of opinion as simply the result of the clients' lack of taste or proper respect for his genius. He was certainly not alone—famous architects often come across as patient sufferers who believe that their burden is to do creative work for lesser mortals who need to be protected from their own misguided impulses. We have personally worked with several high-profile, highly arrogant architects, including one who rather startlingly announced in a meeting with clients that listening to any requests from the planned occupants of his creation "would completely destroy the concept of the building."

We should add, though, that arrogance is not the inevitable companion of genius in the creative arts. Examples such as Monet and Matisse in painting or Isaac Stern and Stephane Grappelli in music each represent maximum achievement with minimum self-inflation. They are notable for not only being at the tops of their fields, but also for continuing to explore, learn from those around them and grow in their craft to very advanced ages. Unlike many high achievers, they seemed to be totally uninterested in resting on their laurels and having the little people repeatedly tell them how great they had been

Science and Medicine

We all know that it takes tremendous amounts of skill, training, and experience to become a world-renowned figure in medicine, medical research, or science. A certain amount of the "all knowing, always right" attitude of many physicians may represent a coping mechanism for the burden of their responsibilities— many of their judgments can truly be said to be matters of life and death. In addition, traditional medical schools still provide a heavy component of "You're No.1" socialization to their prospective doctors. Even though there generally is a lack of mutuality built into the roles within the medical profession, it does not inherently require that physicians assume the right to behave arrogantly toward both patients and others in the health care professions. Yet it is sad to hear the reports by nurses of the dismissive treatment they receive from many doctors in hospital settings. Two good examples: a movie entitled, *The Doctor* (starring William Hurt) about a skilled but arrogant surgeon who becomes humble and caring after discovering he has cancer and is a patient himself. The contrast in behavior is stark. Another such example is the British TV comedy series, *Doc Martin*, where a brilliant physician is both arrogant and interpersonally distant. The show is entertaining because it is only a mild exaggeration of reality.

The negative impact on medical team effectiveness caused by doctor arrogance was recently highlighted in a nurse's *New York Times'* Op-Ed piece about arrogant doctor bullying: " Indeed, every nurse has a story like mine, and most have several. A nurse I know, attempting to clarify and order, was told ' When you have an M.D. after your name you can talk to me.' A doctor dismissed another's complaint by simply saying, 'I'm important.' When a doctor thoughtlessly dresses down a nurse in front of patients or their families, it's not just a personal affront, it's an incredible distraction, taking our minds away from our patients, focusing them instead on how powerless we are. That said, the most damaging bullying is not flagrant and does not fit the stereotype of a surgeon having a tantrum in the operating room. It is passive, like not answering pages or phone calls, and tends toward the subtle: condescension rather than outright abuse, and aggressive or sarcastic remarks rather than straightforward insults."[49] She goes on to describe the blocks to communication, reduced teamwork and subsequent potential and actual errors that occur as a result. It may be one of the arenas where the risks of arrogant behavior are highest in terms of life-or-death impact.

We once had a client who was a very well-known research scientist in biotechnology. He joined one of our client firms from a position in academia. Almost immediately, he began to alienate people by making remarks about how his graduate assistants could turn out better work than his listeners were producing. In fact, he began to refer to his subordinates as "my post-docs", a demeaning reference. Within a year, almost no one in the client organization would have anything to do with this man, and he could not understand why he was being shunned! He really didn't think of himself as arrogant, but merely as truly better than everyone else, so he wrote off their rejection of him as simply the carping of people who were jealous.

We know of another company-founding physician who believes that because of his medical prowess, he also is an expert in finance, marketing, business development, and whatever else requires decisions in the flow of company life. It is very hard for those who work for him (whom he hired for their expertise in these fields) to have influence in the face of his exaggerated opinion of himself. The collective capabilities in the system are therefore wasted, and its capacity is limited to his personal best in any area, and no better.

Admiral Hyman Rickover was a brilliantly arrogant scientist who headed the nuclear navy for many years. Stories about his arrogant behavior are legendary. Nevertheless, he was highly respected and admired for his expertise, if not for his style of behavior.

The Law

Lawyer jokes abound because so many lawyers seem to ooze arrogance as a basic requisite for the role. Clearly some of it is posturing for the press (William Kunstler, F. Lee Bailey, Johnnie Cochran), but much of it is for real. Much of students' experience in law school is aimed at strengthening their ability to win arguments independent of the realities of the situation; those who can be most persuasive are the ones who get rewarded.

The lawyer's struggle to maintain perspective was poignantly portrayed in the movie "Regarding Henry." Harrison Ford plays a lawyer who got shot, recovered and found that his values and his view of the point of his life had changed. He no longer wanted to behave in an arrogant manner, nor could he stand arrogant people.

"*Let me through. I'm a lawyer.*"

Higher Education

Although college presidents are pulled by many conflicting interests, they are still essentially the heads of substantial empires. As such they are subject to all of the usual "top-dog" pressures toward arrogance, and many succumb. John Silber, the former president of Boston University, is probably as good an example as can be found, since he appeared (at least in his public utterances) to divide the world into people who agreed with his opinions and unenlightened ones. When someone disagreed with him, the usual response was not to discuss the content of the issue, but simply to dismiss the dissenter as "second-rate." This was presumably because no first-raters could possibly come to a different conclusion than he had.

But again, the pressures don't automatically determine the outcome. In the example we cited in Chapter 7, John Coleman, the former president of Haverford College, took a year off to do manual labor as a way of reestablishing his perspective and his sense of honesty about the world and his place in it. He recognized that his president's role was tending to constrict his experiences into a smaller and smaller circle of self-reinforcing activities that were designed not to challenge his assumptions or stretch his style.[50]

Sports

The arena of professional sports has seen an explosion in success, fame, money, and general adulation of the fans of whatever sport is at issue. It's only natural that such a fast track would breed (and attract) those who believe that they are truly the chosen people. The role of team owner seems to be a particularly fertile one for arrogance, spawning such stars as George Steinbrenner (baseball), Mark Cuban (basketball) and Jerry Jones (football). Star players can get caught up in their own press releases (e.g., Deion Sanders, Dennis Rodman, Terrell Owens and LeBron James, who famously announced that he was "taking his talents to South Beach"), and even basketball referees or major league umpires can begin to behave as if they had been blessed with an infallibility that is denied to mere mortals. The way the society reacts to outstanding ability and performance of star players makes it easy for them to behave arrogantly. They typically have enormous salaries, endorsement deals, and people surrounding them who are full of admiration and willing to do anything for them.

Sometimes arrogance appears in a person's behavior after having achieved a truly stunning performance—as apparently happened after Michael Phelps won seven gold medals in swimming. People reported that his subsequent behavior was very different from his (presumed) real nature and the way he had behaved for years prior to his amazing feat. The same can be said about Bode Miller, whose arrogance following his wins in world competitive skiing races included refusing to work with the U.S. ski team, and traveling in a private motor home surrounded by admirers.

The opposite of the "star syndrome" has been demonstrated many times where coaches and players have developed a finely tuned culture of collaboration that pays off. One dramatic example was the stunning gold medal won by the U.S. hockey team at the 1980 Winter Olympics. In that case, the players and coach built the group into an incredibly tight knit team where each player not only did his best, but they were able to enhance one another's abilities through their extraordinary teamwork. They won despite not having been rated as having much of a chance in the pre-tournament speculations. The same thing often happens in post-season football games between a championship team and a team made up of all-stars; the championship team wins most often because they have built tremendous trust throughout the season.

In the examples used in this chapter, the people usually have an element of true greatness about them; they are brilliant, insightful, supremely dedicated, artistically gifted, etc. Being on the cutting edge or breaking through old conventions requires a determination that keeps them focused amid the noise of doubts, fears, and limited viewpoints. But there is also a tendency for this focus to create dismissive relationships where the great one rejects, a priori, others' views and values, and expects them simply to nod and accept whatever wisdom is being dispensed. This may help the gifted ones maintain focus in some situations where collaboration is not critical, and it can lead to true innovations. But in complex situations that require concerted effort and resources beyond any one person, this is not a very good design. Outcomes are obviously limited to the best that the star has to offer, and often even less than that, since the necessity to maintain the image of superiority can push against taking creative risks. Some of the judgments will also inevitably be wrong, no matter what the star's or the fans' beliefs.

CHAPTER 10

Putting It In Perspective

So having explored the concept and experience of executive arrogance from a number of different angles, where does this leave us? We began thinking about writing this book quite a few years ago and worked on ideas and draft chapters off and on over the years. When the financial crisis of 2007-2009 occurred and we began to see articles and books on the topic appear, we were spurred into serious action because so much of the problem actually was caused by unbelievable corporate arrogance. When an arrogant executive is in a position of power, that person's entire organization tends to become arrogant as well. As if arrogant behavior isn't bad enough, the negative effects of the arrogance are multiplied enormously when it becomes institutional in nature. In the last two years, a number of books and a myriad of magazine and newspaper articles have been written that detail the inner workings of organizations that had solid reputations and strong positive public images as they participated in causing the financial crisis—in particular, Bear Stearns, Lehman Brothers and AIG. The Federal government (Treasury Department, Federal Reserve, White House economic advisors) also acted arrogantly, refusing to listen to many warnings about the coming disaster—from 2000 to 2006. The common thread in these accounts is the evidence of executive arrogance—people in key leadership positions who were so sure of their own point(s) of view that they simply were unwilling to listen to anyone who thought differently.

As stated in the introduction to Edmund Andrews book, *Busted*, "Everybody had a reason for getting in trouble. The brokers and deal-makers were scoring huge commissions. The condo flippers were aiming for quick profits. Ordinary home buyers wanted to own their first houses, bigger houses, or vacation houses. Some were greedy, some were desperate, and some were deceived. That said, this crisis would not have been possible without breathtaking cynicism on the part of the brainiest people and biggest institutions in American finance. This is a fairly simple story about how a lot of really smart people embraced and proselytized for a lot of inexcusable hogwash. This was a debacle that stemmed from deep-seated rot and corroded ethics in our financial system."[51] And to that, we would add only that it all stemmed from *incredible* institutional arrogance. As the whole thing came unraveled, all the principal players were claiming that they were ignorant or unaware of what was happening!

Yet the signs had been visible ever since the late 1990s when a hedge fund named Long-Term Capital Management (LTCM) experienced a meltdown. Its stock price went from $5.50 in May of 1998 to $0.50 in September of that year. They company took unprecedented risks and experienced unprecedented losses (it was leveraged greater than 100 to 1). "Long-Term had calculated with mathematical certainly that it was unlikely to lose more than $35 million on any single day, but dropped $553 million—15%

of its capital—on one Friday in August."⁵² Interestingly, the institutions that came to Long-Term's rescue were the same ones that experienced similar collapses ten years later, including Bear Stearns, Lehman Brothers, Merrill Lynch, Citibank and others, despite clear warnings throughout the decade. "Alan Greenspan freely admitted that by orchestrating a rescue of Long-Term, the Fed had encouraged future risk takers and perhaps increased the odds of a future disaster."⁵³ It is our opinion that one reason that the warnings were not heard nor acted upon was the arrogance of those institutions and their leaders.

As long as 4 years before the economic crisis, credible and informed people had been warning publicly that the situation was untenable, and no one paid any attention to them. In fact, within Merrill Lynch, its chief North American Economist, David Rosenberg, in August of 2004 warned that housing prices were wildly out of sync with fundamental values. "Rosenberg's warnings would turn out to be deadly accurate. But in retrospect, what made them striking was that Merrill Lynch's top executives disregarded them entirely."⁵⁴ Warren Buffett, in a letter to shareholders in 2002, called derivatives "toxic" and said they were "time bombs" that were expanding unchecked and could cause a chain reaction of financial disaster.⁵⁵

What follows are three illustrations of the extreme arrogance exhibited throughout the financial crisis.

Regarding Long-Term Capital Management

> "The heart of the fund was a group of brainy, Ph.D.-certified arbitrageurs. Many of them had been professors. Two had won the Nobel Prize. All of them were very smart. And they knew they were very smart. Long-Term's secretive, close-knit mathemati-

cians had treated everyone else on Wall Street with utter disdain. Merrill Lynch, the firm that had brought Long-Term into being, had long tried to establish a profitable, mutually rewarding relationship with the fund. So had many other banks. But Long-Term had spurned them. The professors had been willing to trade on their terms and only on theirs—not to meet the banks halfway. The bankers did not like it that the once haughty Long-Term was pleading for their help."[56]

Regarding Lehman Brothers:

"If only they had listened—Dick Fuld and his president, Joe Gregory. Three times they were hit with the irredeemable logic of three of the cleverest financial brains on Wall Street—those of Mike Gelband, global head of fixed income, Alex Kirk, global head of distressed trading research and sales, and Larry McCarthy, head of distressed bond trading. Each and every one of them laid it out, from way back in 2005, that the real estate market was living on borrowed time and that Lehman Brothers was headed directly for the biggest subprime iceberg even seen, and with the wrong men on the bridge. Dick and Joe turned their backs all three times."[57]

Regarding Enron:

"It seemed that within days the company started to come unraveled, and the fraud, the false accounting designed to inflate their revenue, came glaringly into light. That did it—the stock, which had been trading that fall at $85, crashed to 30 cents once it became obvious what was happening. The scandal took down the hitherto respected accounting firm of Arthur Andersen, the fifth largest in the world. The colossal deception was so convoluted that it managed to provide the illusion of billion-dollar profits when the company was actually losing money....Many insiders knew what was happening and began wholesale selling of stocks before the crash....Skilling and his cohorts kept talking up the stock, swearing to God it was going to $130 or even $150....Kenneth Lay, the founder and chairman, was as guilty as Skilling, and, if anything, even worse in his demeanor, assuring shareholders who were losing money on a daily basis that all would be well if they just kept their nerve. Even his wife, Linda, was unloading the stock while he continued to exhort the supporters of the corporation to keep the faith."[58]

As we said at the beginning of the book, arrogant behavior in leaders is certainly nothing new, having been with us throughout recorded history. It seemed to be mostly taken for granted, as if it was the price to pay for being led by people (mostly men) who were both intellectually brilliant and emotionally able to shoulder daunting responsibilities that would cow more humble folk. In other words, people around them didn't particularly like it, but assumed that it was just the way it had to be.

There also seemed to be an assumption that it was good enough—that there were irritations and costs but on the whole arrogant leadership behavior got the enterprise where it was supposed to go. But there have been many spectacular misfires in the past decade, including Enron, Lehman Brothers, AIG, much of the rest of Wall Street and the banking and insurance industries, not to mention the US automakers and a number of high-profile technology companies. In all of these instances, there was unwavering grasping onto business models that top leaders held to be exempt from challenge by people either within or outside their organizations.

The point is that today's environment doesn't provide enough slack to be able to survive with closed-loop thinking. Things change too quickly, communications happen too continuously, and healthy organizations need to be able to learn, test, challenge and adapt on a more or less continuous basis. The arrogant stance of "I know I'm right, so don't bother me with facts," is too costly, too slow to adapt, and unsustainable in challenging or difficult times. We're not sure whether making-do ever really worked very well, but it's abundantly clear that it doesn't today.

One of our main themes has been that we don't think it's very helpful to treat arrogance as simply a personality trait, immutably tied to a person due to their predispositions and life experiences. There is no doubt that there are people who tend to feel that they are always right, or at least must always "look" right, in order to feel that they meet their own standards. As we have also discussed, there are life situations that will also reinforce this view of oneself as the fount of all received wisdom: fawning parents, entourages of hangers-on, and subordinates who want only to be seen as supportive and agreeable no matter what the topic. These are clearly factors in shaping how executives and other leaders respond to situations, but the point is that these experiences are contributors but not determiners of leaders' stances or choices in specific situations.

There is much more scope for getting unstuck from our own rigid styles in dealing with others if we focus on *arrogant behavior* as a pattern of actions that we could actually influence in a meaningful and timely way. Our personalities may predispose us toward arrogance, but this doesn't mean that we must always behave arrogantly in critical situations. With this in mind, we have tried to focus on the recognition of choice points as a means of having a wider repertoire of possible actions and a more beneficial impact on those around us. Arrogantly dismissing others as unable to provide any ideas or information of worth is a way of closing the books and having to rely solely on whatever you already know and believe. This might serve you well in some instances, but it drastically lowers the odds of dealing with a changing reality and discovering other relevant inputs when the situation does not fit your pre-conceived images.

Assuming that you already know all the answers in advance strikes us as simply a bad strategy if you're leading a complex organization through difficult times. (Or even normal times, for that matter.) It makes it hard get the best out a presumably competent team that you have assembled, and it also somewhat trusts to luck that you hold all the information and wisdom to solve problems. The closed nature of such a stance means that "reality" will be defined as whatever you already believe, even when much better information is available if you are more able to listen and really hear it. Just as one of the important roles of leaders is to shape effective processes in the system, it's also important for leaders to shape their own processes so they are not creating a self-fulfilling world-view that determines actions with no reality-checks allowed. You may be doing many things in a given interaction: demonstrating your intelligence, expressing your power, trying to instill a sense of awe in your subordinates, etc. but the list must also include making sound choices that further the interests of the enterprise you are leading.

We have suggested that a crucial step is simply recognizing that your leadership behaviors in different situations can be (and generally are) chosen, and not simply reflex actions. Beyond recognition, we have suggested that several attitudes can help you have a wider range of choices available. *Genuine humility* is obviously one stance that can help you hear others. This is no doubt easier to say than to effect consciously, since feeling humble is exactly what an arrogantly-behaving executive tends not to do. As we suggested, building some relationships where you get honest feedback can help with this, as does actively trying to learn from choices that had negative or mixed consequences.

Likewise, a strong sense of *curiosity* is a natural promoter of getting outside one's own views or circle in critical times. This is a bit like humility, since it's hard to know how you turn on curiosity if you don't have it. However, in our experience this is actually an attitude that can be consciously influenced. As we suggested in Chapter 7, it is promoted by thinking of oneself as a constant learner. When leaders set themselves specific tasks to keep them seeking information beyond their current world-views, they can experience enough success in discovering information that was not predictable to learn from the practice. Over time, they develop a more natural tendency to accept the possibility of surprises, to wonder about things and to try to find out what they don't know or even if they don't know about something.

A third quality that serves as an antidote to arrogant behavior is having a robust *sense of humor*. This is very connected to the first two qualities: one tends to remain more humble if they can see the funny or odd sides to unexpected events and situations, especially ones to which they have contributed. And we suspect that a sense of curiosity is strongly correlated with a sense of humor, by simply opening someone up to see more than one interpretation of an action or event—especially the unintended consequences that don't match the official version of what should be happening. This is probably the least fruitful area for improvement through practice, since a sense of humor (or lack thereof) is shaped by one's ability not to take things too seriously or have to maintain one consistent view of one's self as always correct and competent. Having said this, it does suggest that practicing humility could open up the humor side a bit.

The fourth factor that helps rein-in arrogant executive behavior is a strong *commitment to the cause or enterprise*. This doesn't mean that arrogant leaders tend to feel that they are uncommitted—in most cases they believe that their very commitment requires them to rely exclusively on their own abilities, since the outcome is too important to be left to others who are inherently less qualified. What we have suggested is simply that real commitment to good outcomes means consciously choosing personal processes that include reality-checks that get outside one's own bubble in order to maximize the probability of spotting important information or approaches that don't reside in oneself.

The last factor is a *strong commitment to the people around you*. This means that you recognize that as a leader with considerable power to affect peoples' lives you are a major contributor to the environment or climate in which your peers and subordinates operate. If every interchange has to demonstrate your personal brilliance, people either choose to leave or they stay and have few opportunities to develop their own abilities or competence. Conversely, if you can set a tone of listening, exploration and valuing a range of ideas and inputs, people tend to raise their own level of commitment and to grow in the process.

If one follows these strategies, what difference does it make? We have also hopefully made the case that reducing the level and frequency of arrogant executive behavior has several very important outcomes for the organization. For one, the system's processes for reality testing, for both inside and outside information, should be much more effective. This in turn should lead to better processes of problem spotting and problem solving, both because more accurate data are being considered and because a range of solutions can be considered beyond the preferred approach of the leader alone. We strongly believe that these enable an organization's leaders and members to do much better at learning from experience, so that new patterns and solutions become quickly incorporated into the system's lore and processes.

Ultimately, each of these effects mean that the system is better at quickly adapting to changed conditions, which in these times often means the difference between survival and disappearing from the scene.

We won't repeat the considerable costs of not doing well with these processes, since several of the previous chapters have described the short and long term consequences of a system that is stuck in a pattern of executive arrogance and rigid unwillingness to engage with a spirit of inquiry. Costs are incurred by demoralization or loss of important personnel and by placing limitations on adaptive responses that are built into the system. It's also just not much fun to have to operate in such a climate for any length of time.

As we noted in Chapter 6, if your problems with the downsides of arrogance stem less from your own behavior and more with trying to cope with a boss or another colleague, your options are somewhat more limited. You can't exercise the same control over others' behavior that you can with your own, so exerting some influence over the process is the more likely alternative. Challenging repeated arrogant behavior in your boss can be a risky venture, but if the stakes are high enough, you may be able to get their attention and get them to consider a broader range of views (others' as well as your own). In general, however, we think that you're more likely to have an effect if you can frame the issue as systemic and not personal. Arrogant behavior is a pattern that should be addressed as part of the social climate, since presumably it's not a good thing if anyone in power tends to dismiss any ideas other than their own. It's much more powerful in the long run to think about effective processes and the norms or policies that will support them than it is to treat arrogance as a series of "fixes" to individuals who are deficient.

In effect, this is basically a matter of doing something that should be done anyway: creating and maintaining a working climate that respects everyone, values their inputs while challenging issues and views of reality, and discourages dismissive or demeaning behavior by anyone. It's beyond a leader/executive/boss issue—it's really a human relations issue. If it's approached this way as a group concern, you don't even need to use the term "arrogance," which tends to produce defensiveness and often more arrogant behavior by dismissing the possibility. The avowed goal would simply be to foster a healthy climate that gives and gets the best from everyone.

To sum up, some of the options for trying to cope with or remove the constraints of arrogant executive behavior have focused on testing and shaping one's own personal stances, while others have suggested ways to cope with an arrogant or overbearing boss or colleague. Both of these are aimed at creating more flexible, adaptive situations where the best can be obtained from both yourself and others around you. We also suggested the Arrogance Quotient (AQ) Test as one simple way we have found to get a reading on ourselves and possibly set some goals about new stances to take, especially in situations that have high-stakes risks and potential outcomes. We don't mean to present it as a high-precision scientific instrument (and we will disavow all knowledge of your actions if you try to use it as such), but rather as a reminder of how to step outside yourself and see your impact in situations where others may not be free or willing to do that for you.

In the end, we probably could sum up the dilemma of the arrogant leader in one thought: you may be extremely smart and competent, but if you tend systematically to dismiss the observations and ideas of those around you on the basis that you always know best, you actually are following a dumb strategy that reduces the probability of spotting new information or ideas, building support for your ideas, building the self-worth and confidence of the others, and getting to decisions that fit the realities of the times. We think almost everybody has the capacity to do and be better, and today's leaders owe it to themselves and others to make the effort to do so.

Endnotes

CHAPTER 1

1. Bethany McLean and Peter Elkind, *The Smartest Guys in the Room: The Amazing Rise and Scandalous Fall of Enron*, New York: Portfolio (Penguin Group), 2003, p.28
2. Thomas Friedman, *The World is Flat*, New York: Farrar, Straus and Giroux, 2005
3. Malcolm Gladwell, "Cocksure: Banks, Battles and the Psychology of Overconfidence," *The New Yorker*, July 27, 2009, pp. 24-28
4. Lawrence MacDonald and Patrick Robinson, *The Colossal Failure of Common Sense*, New York: Crown Publishing, 2009
5. William D. Cohen, *House of Cards: A Tale of Hubris and Wretched Excess on Wall Street*, New York: Doubleday, 2009
6. Two PBS Frontline programs clearly detail these signs: "The Meltdown," February 7, 2009, and "The Warning," October 20, 2009, show clearly how arrogance prevented the warnings from being taken seriously by those in charge.

CHAPTER 2

7. *Wall Street Journal*, Wednesday, March 17, 2004
8. David Brooks, "The Gospel According to Mel Gibson," *New York Times*, July 15, 2010
9. Wendy T. Behary, *Disarming the Narcissist: Surviving & Thriving with the Self-Absorbed*, Oakland, CA: New Harbinger Publications, 2008.
10. Samuel Grier, *Narcissism in the Workplace*, Mira Publishing, 2008
11. Alexander Lowen, *Narcissism: Denial of the True Self*, New York: Touchstone (Simon and Schuster), 2004
12. Kenneth N. Wexley and Stanley B. Silverman, *Working Scared: Achieving Success in Trying Times*, New York: John N. Wiley & Sons (Jossey-Bass), 1993
13. Jean M. Twenge, and W. Keith Campbell, *The Narcissism Epidemic*, New York: Free Press (Simon & Schuster), 2009

CHAPTER 3

14. Barbara Ehrenreich, *Nickel and Dimed: On (Not) Getting By in America*, New York: Holt and Company, 2001
15. Robert S. McNamara and Brian VanDeMark, *In Retrospect: The Tragedy and Lessons of Vietnam*, New York, Times Books, 1995
16. Deborah Shapley, *Promise and Power: The Life and Times of Robert McNamara*, Boston: Little Brown, 1993
17. In the biography of Warren Buffet, *The Snowball* by Alice Schroeder, New York, Random House, 2008, he is quoted as having acted as a whistle blower on these kinds of financial operations as early as 1991 (p.570-571, p.608, p.618) concerning the near collapse of Salomon. He tried again in 1998 during the failure of the hedge fund, Long-Term Capital Management (p. 663-664).
18. Roger Lowenstein, *When Genius Failed: The Rise and Fall of Long-Term Capital Management*, New York: Random House, 2002

CHAPTER 4

19. Rosabeth Moss Kanter, *Work Pray Love*, Harvard Business Review Column, December, 2010.
20. Fritz Steele, "The Ecology of the New Executive Team, in *Leader to Leader*, Fall, 2009, p. 22.
21. *Ibid.*, p. 24.

CHAPTER 5

22. Bethany McLean and Peter Elkind, *The Smartest Guys in the Room: The Amazing Rise and Scandalous Fall of Enron*, New York: Portfolio (Penguin Group), 2003, p.140
23. Lou Dubose and Jake Bernstein, Vice: *Dick Cheney and the Highjacking of the American Presidency*, New York: Random House, 2006, p.167
24. George Packer, *The Assassins' Gate*, New York: Farrar, Strauss & Giroux, 2005, p. 117
25. Packer, p. 117
26. McLean and Elkind, p. 257
27. McLean and Elkind, p. 121
28. McLean and Elkind, p. 285-286

CHAPTER 6

29. Eric Berne, *Games People Play*, New York: Grove Press, 1964, especially chapters 1-3
30. Theresa Brown, "Physician, Heel Thyself," *New York Times*, Sunday, May 8, 2011
31. Rachel Lehmann-Haupt & Warren St. John, "Corporate Bad Guys Make Many Seek the Road Less Traveled," *New York Times*, Sunday, July 21, 2002

CHAPTER 7

32. David H. Maister, Charles H. Green, and Robert M. Galford, *The Trusted Advisor*, New York: Touchstone (Simon & Schuster), 2000
33. John R. Coleman, *Blue-Collar Journal, A College President's Sabbatical*, Philadelphia, PA: Lippincott, 1974
34. Adam Bryant, *The Corner Office: Indispensable and Unexpected Lessons from CEO's on How to Lead and Succeed*, New York: Times Books, 2011

CHAPTER 8

35. Fritz Steele and Stephen Jenks, *The Feel of the Workplace: Understanding and Improving Organizational Climate*, Reading, Massachusetts, Addison-Wesley, 1977
36. Lawrence MacDonald and Patrick Robinson, *The Colossal Failure of Common Sense*, New York: Crown Publishing (2009), p. 70.
37. L. McDonald, p.2
38. David H. Maister, Charles H. Green and Robert M. Galford, *The Trusted Advisor*, New York: Free Press, 2000, p. 52.
39. Edgar H. Schein, *DEC is Dead; Long Live DEC*, San Francisco: Berrett Koehler, 2003
40. Peter S. Goodman, "In Case of Emergency: What not to Do," *New York Times*, Sunday, August 23, 2010. p.Bu6
41. The site for the video is: http://gethuman.com/video
42. P. Goodman, p. Bu6
43. "Murdoch Empire Faces New Scandal Potentially Far More Damaging", Arthur Bright, Christian Science Monitor, March 30, 2012
44. "Rebecca Brooks Arrest: Phone-hacking Scandal Isn't Going to Fade", Robert Marquand, Christian Science Monitor, March 13, 2012
45. P. Goodman. P. Bu7

CHAPTER 9

46. "Air Sununu Grounded", *Washington Post*, June 1, 1991
47. "The White House: A Bad Case of the Perks", *Time*, July 1, 1991
48. Frank Bruni, "Self-Adoration Reaches Newt Heights," *New York Times*, Dec. 18, 2011, p. sr3
49. T. Brown, p. wk. 8
50. John R. Coleman: *Blue-Collar Journal: A College President's Sabbatical*, Philadelphia, PA: Lippincott, 1974

CHAPTER 10

51. Edmund L. Andrews, *Busted: Life Inside the Great Mortgage Meltdown*, New York: W.W. Norton, 2009, p. x-xii.
52. Roger Lowenstein, *When Genius Failed*, New York: Penguin Press, 2000, p.147
53. Lowenstein, p.229
54. Andrews, p.22

55. Alice Schroeder, *The Snowball: Warren Buffett and the Business of Life*, New York: Bantam Books (Random House), 2008, pg 733
56. Lowenstein, p.xix-xx
57. Lawrence MacDonald and Patrick Robinson, *The Colossal Failure of Common Sense*, New York: Crown Publishing (2009), p.2.
58. Andrews, p.70

Index

active listening, 73
adaptability, arrogance and, xi, 2, 54-55, 137-138
AIG, 1, 29, 133, 137
Albany Times Union, 104
ambiguity, avoidance of, 49
Amin, Idi, 13
Andrews, Edmund, 134
anxiety, 3, 49, 55
AOL (America Online), 4
Apple Computer, 107
  corporate image of, 109
arrogance
  active listening and, 73
  antidotes to, 84-98
  in the arts, 125-126
  benefits to leader of, 48-50
  career paths affected by, 62-66
  characteristics confused with, 10, 14
  as closed-mindedness, 10, 137
  costs of, 117, 142
  dangers of, ix-x, 8, 137-139
  dealing with, xii, xiii, 68-83
  distancing tendency of, 52
  energy associated with, 59
  exploiting, 56
  in fiction, 11, 13
  in higher education, 130
  hindering information gathering, 52-54
  hindering learning, 54-55, 67
  hindering teamwork, 60
  inflexibility of, xi, 2, 61-63, 137-138
  institutional, 7, 99-121
  interpersonal effects of, 56-57
  intelligence and, 25-26
  in the law, 129
  manifestations of, 24
  in medicine, 126-128
  in modern conditions, 4
  narcissistic nature of, 22
  negative consequences of, 51-68
  in negotiation, 56
  overconfidence in, 7, 10-12
  in politics, 13, 121-125
  public exposure to, 1
  vs. reality, x, 53-54, 62, 139
  resentment caused by, 57-58, 61
  resistance to, 51
  rewards of, 59-60
  risk-taking and, 58-59
  in the sciences, 128
  in sports, 130-132
  strength and, 59-60
  symbols of, 32-34
  as systemic problem, 80
  technical expertise and, 45-47
arrogance quotient (AQ), 86-87, 143
arrogant behaviors, 20
  circumstance and, 28-31
  factors in eliciting, 21-22
  inherited, 27
  as learned behaviors, 25-27, 138
  organizational effects of, 58-59, 137-138
  origins of, 24-25, 89-90
  voluntariness of, 20, 23, 138
Arthur Andersen, 136
arts, arrogance in the, 125-126
attention, reinforced by arrogance, 50
Audi, corporate arrogance at, 110, 114-115
automobile, as status symbol, 36-37, 103
automotive industry, 109-110, 114-115

Bailey, F. Lee, 129
banking industry, 6-7, 133-135
Battle, Kathleen, 125
Bear Stearns, 29, 103, 133, 135
Berne, Eric, 74
Blagojevich, Rod, 1
Blankfein, Lloyd, 29
Blue Collar Journal, 94
BP Gulf oil spill, 114
Brent, David, 15

INDEX | 151

Brooks, David, 22
Brooks, Rebecca, 117
Brown, Teresa, 79
Bruni, Frank, 123
Bryant, Adam, 97
Bryant, Kobe, 29
Buffett, Warren, 28, 38, 135
Bunker, Archie, 11, 13
Burns, Brad, 109
Bush, George H. W., 122
Bush, George W., 27, 123
Busted, 134

Callas, Maria, 125
career limiting move, 74-75
Carter, Jimmy, 124
Case, Steve, 4
certainty, provided by arrogance, 49, 55
change
  adaptation to, 17-18
  factors in, 2
change project, 71-75
changing phase, 72
Cheney, Dick, 1, 51, 123
Citibank, 135
climate
  and arrogance, 100-102
  rhetoric caused by, 100-101
closed-mindedness, 10
clothing, as status symbol, 44-45, 102-103
Cochran, Johnnie, 129
Cohen, William D., 7
Coleman, John, 94, 130
collaboration
  intergroup, 104-106
  team, 105
The Colossal Failure of Common Sense, 7
commiseration, 75-76
commitment
  to a cause or enterprise, 140-141
  to people, 141
communication, hindered by arrogance, 61
Compaq, 107
competition
  in institutional arrogance, 101
  institutional arrogance hindered by, 112-113;
  nature of, 16
complexity, management of, 16, 18
compliance, provided by arrogance, 49
computer industry, 107-108
confidence, vs. overconfidence, 8, 11
control, arrogance and, 49
coping with arrogance, xii, xiii, 142-143
  in context, 80-83
  dangers of fighting fire with fire, 78-79
  data-centered approach to, 76-77
  mediation, 75
  mounting a change project, 71-75
  picking your battles, 70
  taking your best shot, 70-71
coping with one's own arrogance, 84-85, 143-144
  assessment, 86-87
  environmental causes, 90-91
  humor in, 97-98
  learning from experience, 88-89
  manifestations, 91-92
  outcomes, 92
  process plan for, 92-93
  role management in, 93-95
  seeking objective view, 96
  self-curiosity, 97
  therapeutic process in, 89-90
The Corner Office, 97
Countrywide Financial, 29
CP/M operating system, 107
creativity, hindered by arrogance, 66-67
credibility, building, 78
Cuban, Mark, 131
culture, management of, 16, 18
curiosity, importance of, 97, 139-140
customers, arrogance toward, 108-112

data-centered approach to arrogance, 76-77
de Gaulle, Charles, 123
dealers, relations with, 112
deregulation, corporate arrogance hindered by, 113
derivatives, 135
Digital Equipment Corporation (DEC), 106-107
Doc Martin, 127
The Doctor, 127
DOS operating system, 107

economic cycles, 3
ECT, 60
educational level, as status symbol, 105
electronic media, 4
English, Paul, 111
Enron, 1, 3, 50, 60, 62, 83, 103, 136-137
entitlement, 24, 27
ethics, and institutional arrogance, 116-118
executive dining room, 40-41, 103
executive washroom, 41, 103
Exxon, corporate arrogance at, 102
Exxon Enterprises, 102
Exxon Valdez oil spill, 115-116

Fastow, Andy, 50
financial crisis of 2007 et seqq., 133-134

institutional arrogance and, 134
prelude to, 134-135
roots of, 6-7
flat organizational structure, 118
Ford, Gerald, 124
Ford, Harrison, 129
Ford Motor Company, 28
form follows function, 39-40
Friedman, Thomas, 5
Fuld, Richard, Jr., 29, 103, 136
furniture
    form follows function, 39-40
    as status symbol, 38, 102

Games People Play, 74
Gekko, Gordon, 11
Gelband, Mike, 136
General Motors
    corporate arrogance at, 115
    corporate image of, 109
Gervais, Ricky, 15
gethuman.com, 111
Gingrich, Newt, 123
Gladwell, Malcolm, 6
globalization, 4
Goldman Sachs, 29, 119
Goodman, Peter, 114, 119
Grapelli, Stephane, 126
Greenspan, Alan, 123, 135
Gregory, Joe, 136

Hayward, Tony, 114
higher education, arrogance in, 130
Hitler, Adolf, 13
home, as status symbol, 37-38
Horowitz. Vladimir, 125
House of Cards, 7
House Post Office, check overdraft scandal of, 122
housing bubble, 134-135
humility, 139
humor
    in coping with arrogance, 97-98
    of leader, 140
Hurt, William, 127
Hussein, Saddam, 13

IBM, 10, 1117
    corporate image of, 109, 112-113
    telecommuting in, 34
In Search of Excellence, 107
institutional arrogance, 99-121
    collaboration hindered by, 104-106
    competition hindering, 112-113
    and corporate clients, 108-113
    deregulation hindering, 113
    ethical aspects of, 116-118

    ignoring problems, 111-112
    institutional pride and, 106-108
    meetings and, 100
    organizational climate, 100-102
    organizational limitations of, 118-120
    and outside world, 113-118
    patterns of, 99
    and representatives, 112
    rewarding individual arrogance, 101-102
    and suppliers, 112
    tone set by leader, 102-106
Intel, corporate arrogance at, 111
interdependence, management of, 16
intergroup collaboration, 104-106
iPhone, 110

J. P. Morgan Chase, 83
James, LeBron, 131
Jobs, Steve, 45, 109
Johnson & Johnson, 116
Jones, Jerry, 131
Kirk, Alex, 136
Kissinger, Henry, 122
knowledge-based activities, 4
Kodak, corporate arrogance at, 102
Kozlowski, Dennis, 11, 83
Kunstler, William, 129

law, arrogance in the, 129
Lay, Kenneth, 103, 136-137
leaders
    benefits of arrogance to, 48-50
    characteristics of, 19-20
    and circumstance, 30-31
    commitment to cause of, 140-141
    curiosity in, 139-140
    desirable traits and behaviors in, 139-142
    humility of, 139
    and institutional arrogance, 102-106
    relation of subordinate to, 77-80
    roles of, 15-16
    teaching role of, 15, 55
Lehman Brothers, 1, 29, 103, 133, 135, 136, 137
lifestyle, status and, 37-38
Long-Term Capital Management (LTCM), 134-136

Mark, Rebecca, 59
Matisse, Henri, 126
McCarthy, Larry, 136
McCarthyism, 101
McDonald, Lawrence, 7
McNamara, Robert, 28
mediation, 75

INDEX | 153

medicine, arrogance in, 126-128
meetings, in arrogant climate, 101
Merrill Lynch, 135, 136
Microsoft, 107
Miller, Bode, 131
Mitchell, George, 124
Molinaro, Sam, 103
Monet, Claude, 126
Moore, Michael, 115
Moses, 123
Mugabe, Robert, 13
Murdoch, Rupert, 117

narcissism, 22
negotiation, arrogance in, 56
Netscape, 4
news media, 4
News Corp., 117-118
News of the World, 117
Nixon, Richard, 121-122

Obama, Barack, 124
The Office, 15
Oshry, Barry and Karen, 20
outsourcing, of technical support, 111
overconfidence
    appeal of, 12
    as arrogance, 7, 10-12
    distinguished from confidence, 8, 11
Owens, Terrell, 131

passionate curiosity, 97
Paulson, Henry, 29
Pentium chip, 111
Peters, Tom, 107
Phelps, Michael, 131
Picasso, Pablo, 125
picking your battles, 70
politics, arrogance in, 13, 121-125
Power & Systems Laboratory, 20
    described, 21
process plan, for dealing with arrogance, 92-93

Reagan, Ronald, 123, 124
reality
    arrogance vs., ix-x, 16-17, 139
    testing of, 53-54, 62, 66
reciprocity, norm of, 57
refreezing, 73
Regarding Henry, 129
resentment, of arrogance, 57-58
Rickover, Hyman, 128
ridicule, 100
Robinson, Patrick, 7
Rodman, Dennis, 131
Roethlisberger, Ben, 29

Roger and Me, 115
role management, 93-95
Rosenberg, David, 135
Rubin, Robert, 123
Rumsfeld, Donald, 1, 51, 123

Sanders, Deion, 131
Schein, David, 15
Schwartz, Alan, 103
sciences, arrogance in the, 128
seating, symbolism of, 36
SEI Investments, 39
Shah, Ameet, 82-83
Sheen, Charlie, 29
Silber, John, 130
Skilling, Jeff, 3-4, 60, 61-62, 103, 136-137
Smith, Roger, 115
Soviet Union, arrogance in, 101
sports, arrogance in, 130-132
St. Elsewhere, 43
Stalinism, 101
star syndrome, 130-131
status symbols, 32
    assistants as, 42-44
    automobiles, 36-37
    case study of, 34-35
    dress as, 44-45
    executive dining room and washroom, 40-41
    furniture, 38
    houses and lifestyles, 37-38
    obsoleteness of, 33-34
    seat of power, 36
    technology as, 39-40
    workplace layout and, 39-40, 42
Steelcase, 35
Steinbrenner, George, 131
Stern, Isaac, 126
strength, distinguished from arrogance, 59-60
subordinates
    coping with arrogance, 17-18, 56-58, 77-80
    relations to leaders, 14, 51
    as status symbol, 42-44
sub-prime mortgage lending, 28
success, arrogance and, 50
suckers' walk, 42
Summers, Larry, 123
Sununu, John, 122-123
suppliers, relations with, 112
surprise, management of, 15
suspicion, in institutional arrogance, 101
Swartz, Mark, 11
Szell, George, 125

taking your best shot, 70-71

Teach for America, 83
team collaboration, 105
teamwork, hindered by arrogance, 61
technical expertise
    arrogance and, 45-47
    equated with overall knowledge, 6
technology, as status symbol, 39
telephone call automation, 111
telephone industry, corporate image of, 113
Thatcher, Margaret, 123
360 degree feedback exercise, 72, 88
Time Warner, 4
Toscanini, Arturo, 125
Toyota, corporate arrogance at, 109-110
transparency, 35-36
Truman, Harry, 124
trust, creating, 85
The Trusted Advisor, 85
truth teller, 96
Tyco, 11, 83
Tylenol tampering incident, 116

uncertainty, 3
    arrogance as defense against, 49, 55
    intolerance of, 100
unfreezing, 71-73
United Fund scandal, 1
U.S. Olympic hockey team 1980, 131-132
utility deregulation, 113

values, management of, 16, 18
videoconferencing, status and, 39-40

Wallace, William "Braveheart," 123
Wellington, Duke of, 123
White, Tim, 104
Wolfowitz, Paul, 1, 53, 57, 123
Woods, Tiger, 29
workplace
    furniture in, 38
    status symbols in, 32-35
    transparent, 35-36
The World Is Flat, 5
WorldCom, 109
Wright, Frank Lloyd, 125-126

Zanuck, Daryl, 75

PORTLAND PUBLIC LIBRARY SYSTEM
5 MONUMENT SQUARE
PORTLAND, ME 04101